THE WISDOM OF GOD

To Dick & Carole, Thanks
Just a word to say. Dick
For your ministry @ Scott.
Your labor at CHC & Carole...
Your Tremendous faithfulness
& ministry in our nursery.

Dawo Jeremiah
James 1:5

The Wisdom of God

DAVID JEREMIAH

MOTT MEDIA

THE WISDOM OF GOD

Copyright © by Mott Media, Inc., Publishers

First Edition

Copyedited by Leonard George Goss and Ruth Schenk
Typeset by Karen White, Suzanne DePodesta and Joyce Bohn

Printed in the United States of America
ISBN 0-88062-103-6

CONTENTS

This book is lovingly dedicated to my parents,
Dr. and Mrs. James T. Jeremiah,
who, from my childhood, made known to me the Scriptures
"which are able to make you wise for salvation through faith
which is in Christ Jesus" (2 Tim. 3:15).

FOREWORD

There are two kinds of wisdom—man's kind and God's kind.

There is the wisdom available from professionals in a given field; or the course pursued by someone after careful research and investigation. There is the wisdom that is found in corporate board rooms, the marketplace, and in halls of learning. We marvel at human wisdom when we see what we can produce—automobiles, highway systems, planes, electronics, plastics, even putting a man on the moon. We see the breathtaking increase in knowledge and communication reflected in books and magazines stored in vast libraries and computer memories. All this is marvelous in our eyes.

But there is another kind of wisdom—God's kind. Recognition of God's wisdom comes only in knowing the contents of the Bible, God's word to us—reading and studying it with a prayer for understanding, guidance and proper living.

When we recognize that the heavenly Father is the source of a special kind of wisdom, we can more easily accept biblical teachings which may seem, at least on the surface, contrary to our own nature. God's ways are not man's way. But understanding this is the beginning of living according to God's Word by faith.

David Jeremiah has given us in this book a very thorough contrast of worldly wisdom and God's wisdom. But more than explaining the differences, he has skillfully used Scripture to guide the believer who diligently seeks God's wisdom into a pattern for godly living. Wisdom can be gained for a lifetime of meaningful service and victory over circumstances by acting on the teachings in this book.

The Wisdom of God comes at a time when Christians are being influenced on every hand by secular humanism so contrary to the eternal wisdom of our Father. It will be a valuable asset in the hands of any reader seeking the source of godly wisdom so necessary for every need of life.

Henry Brandt, Ph.D.

PREFACE

It was summer, and for six weeks my family and I were touring the Eastern part of our country participating in Bible conferences and visiting some of our famous American landmarks. To say that we were in transition would be an understatement. I had just resigned from the pastorate of a church that I founded and guided for twelve years. Ultimately we were headed West to assume the leadership of a large well-known church. The decision to make the change had been finalized, and we were certain that it was God who had directed us.

Actually, as we look back, we are amazed at the intensity of our struggle with this decision. I really had not wanted to leave the Midwest, but after almost two years of saying no, I gave into God's plan. Now the decision was behind us, and as we traveled we sensed the relief that always accompanies surrender to God's will.

And yet, at the same time, there were other emotions that we felt as well. It had been excruciatingly difficult to say good-by to so many people that we deeply loved. What made it even more painful was that many of our close friends did not agree with our interpretation of the will of God, and they were deeply hurt that we would leave them for another ministry. The emotions that we felt approximated the stages of grief that people experience when they lose a loved one in death.

Here we were, unplugged from the safety of an environment that felt so secure. And at the same time we were not yet involved in the ministry to which we were called. We were in a place never visited before . . . the place called "In-Between."

The primary emotion of the "in-betweener" is fear, and for the first time in my adult life that feeling took control of my heart. I began to reread all of the promises that I had been given by friends and counselors. I revived the slogan that my father had given me on many occasions: "God's Commandments Are God's Enablements." I knew intellectually that God would never call me to a ministry for which He would not equip me, and yet at the same time, I was frightened and apprehensive. What if I failed? What if I discovered first hand the reality of the "Peter Principle?" Suppose I was being promoted to the level of my own incompetence?

As I battled some of those feelings, a new sense of God's provision began to emerge. This fear of inadequacy was a new experience, but it was to become an important prelude to one of the most crucial chapters in my life. I began to understand what Paul meant when he wrote about strength through weakness. I remembered again that God often stretches us beyond the borders of our own ability in order to teach us the dynamics of dependence.

I always depended upon God but at the same time I was a very confident person. There were times when I wondered where my dependence upon God started and my confident personality ended, but there was no wondering now! My self-assurance evaporated with every day that passed during the period of transition. I now knew that unless God took over completely in my life and ministry I could not possibly succeed. It was precisely at this point that this book was born.

As I searched the Scriptures for direction, I found great hope in the promise of James 1:5: "If any of you lack wisdom, let him ask of God, that giveth to all men liberally, and upbraideth not; and it shall be given him."

If this was a bona fide promise from James, then I could again find confidence. The wisdom of *God* was available to me if I would simply ask.

I ransacked the Bible daily, looking for every shred of truth about God's wisdom. How was it acquired? What did it include? Were there any individuals in the Old or New Testaments who clearly obtained His wisdom? How did they differ from others?

What I found was so thrilling to me personally that by the time I arrived at my new assignment, I *had* to share my discoveries. The principles contained in this book where some of the first truths that I communicated to the people of the Scott Memorial Baptist Church in San Diego.

Almost four years have passed since then. They have been stressful, demanding years, but I now know from experience that these principles do work. I know that I could not have survived the transitional challenges that faced me without the constant provision of God's wisdom. There have been so many times when I did not know what to do . . . so many problems that seemed to have no possible solution. But God's wisdom has *never* failed me, and I am now assured that it never will.

I have great confidence in the directives spelled out in this book. I have even greater confidence in the God who stands behind them.

Before I turn you loose to examine these lessons for yourself, I must say a word of appreciation to those who have believed in this project enough to sacrifice for its completion. My wife, Donna, and our four children, Jan, David, Jennifer and Daniel, have been very encouraging and have not made me feel quilty spending time away from them working on this assignment. Glenda Parker, Jeanne Turk and Sally Wolff all had a part in typing and organizing the material for subsequent editing by Mott Media's editors. Barrie Lyons and Sandy Entner willingly read and reread the manuscript and their valuable suggestions have been so helpful.

Most of all, I am grateful to the people of the Scott Memorial Baptist Church who listened intently as I shared these concepts from the pulpit. It was their initial enthusiasm that encouraged me to write.

"Happy is the man that findeth wisdom, and the man that getteth understanding" (Proverbs 3:13).

David Jeremiah
El Cajon, California
April 12, 1985

Help! I Need Wisdom

Help! I need wisdom. If you've ever prayed, you've certainly prayed that prayer at least once. Parents pray this prayer especially when the uncertain teenage years come along. Businessmen call out to God in these terms when financial reverses come their way. Many pastors I know have made this simple request part of their daily routine. *Help! I need wisdom.* If you sense that need in your life, I think we can learn together how wonderfully open God is to dispensing His wisdom to those who seek Him.

Some years ago, I was challenged to read the book of Proverbs through each month. Since there are thirty-one chapters in the book, it is possible to read a chapter each day and go through the entire collection of wise sayings twelve times a year. Although I have not continued this practice in recent years, I have never been sorry for the extra time spent in the Proverbs of Solomon. One of the early discoveries of my Proverbs study was the many promises God has given to those who seek after and obtain His wisdom.

> Happy is the man that findeth wisdom and the man that getteth understanding. (Proverbs 3:13)

> For wisdom is better than rubies, and all things that may be desired are not to be compared to it. (Proverbs 8:11)

> How much better is it to get wisdom than gold! And to get understanding rather to be chosen than silver. (Proverbs 16:16)

> So shall the knowledge of wisdom be unto thy soul: when thou hast found it, then there shall be a reward, and thy expectation shall not be cut off. (Proverbs 24:14)

> When wisdom entereth into thine heart, and knowledge is pleasant unto thy soul; discretion shall preserve thee, understanding shall keep thee. (Proverbs 2:10-11)

> She is more precious than rubies: and all the things thou canst
> desire are not to be compared unto her. Length of days is in
> her right hand; and in her left hand riches and honour. Her
> ways are ways of pleasantness, and all her paths are peace. She
> is a tree of life to them that lay hold upon her: and happy is
> every one that retaineth her. (Proverbs 3:15-18)

Over and over Solomon says, "Get wisdom." No matter what else
you acquire, be sure to acquire wisdom. Before we start our quest
for wisdom, however, we need to determine exactly what we are
seeking!

What is wisdom? Cooleridge says, "Wisdom is common sense in
an uncommon degree." C. H. Spurgeon defines wisdom as "The
right use of knowledge." Francis Hutchison says it is, "Pursuing
the best ends by the best means." Cicero says, "Wisdom is the
knowledge of things human and divine and the causes by which they
are controlled." Someone, unknown to me, has simply added this
definition: "Wisdom is knowledge using its head."

If I had to choose my favorite secular definition, I think it would
be this one: "Wisdom is doing the right thing without precedent."

All of the above definitions and descriptions of wisdom help us
to focus on our goal, but they all lack a spiritual dimension. It is
not enough for us to have only the wisdom which the world offers.
We need something more than that . . . We need the wisdom dis-
pensed by God Himself.

Spiros Zodiates has defined wisdom like this:

> Wisdom is a synonym . . . of the Word, and it refers to that
> perfection and eternity which is to be found only in God the
> Father, manifested to the world through His Son, the Lord
> Jesus, and existing in the world today only through the Holy
> Spirit . . . The wise man is he who has given himself to Jesus
> Christ, and who, by the help of the Holy Spirit, keeps his
> intellect in submission to the will of God.[1]

In Scripture, wisdom always refers to knowledge of the course of
action that will please God and make life what God wants it to be.
When God promises wisdom, He promises a way of life that is
superior to the way of the world. He guarantees that we will find
that good and acceptable and perfect will of God (Romans 12:2).

There is great misunderstanding as to how this gift of wisdom comes to us. In his book, *Knowing God*, J. I. Packer has used two illustrations that portray two understandings of God's wisdom.

THE OVERALL PLAN OF GOD

Packer's first illustration takes us to a railway station. Here we watch the constant movement of trains in and out of the station. Standing on the end of the platform, our vision and comprehension of the overall working of the train system is limited. However, we are then taken to the magnificent control center where we see a long wall chart with a diagram of the entire system for five miles on either side of the station. We are able, by way of the little lights moving on the track, to locate each piece of equipment and see exactly where it is headed. As we watch the system through the eyes of the men who control it, we are able to understand why trains are stopped and started, diverted and side-tracked. The logic behind every movement is understood because we see the entire picture.[2]

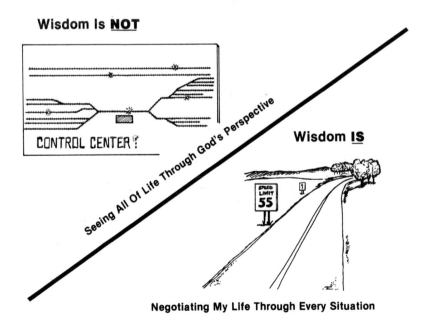

Wisdom Is NOT

CONTROL CENTER

Seeing All Of Life Through God's Perspective

Wisdom IS

SPEED LIMIT 55

Negotiating My Life Through Every Situation

EVERYDAY WISDOM

Packer's second illustration places us inside an automobile. We are learning to drive and are being taught that correct driving is wrapped up in the speed and appropriateness of our reactions to things and the soundness of our judgment in each situation.

We are not concerned with why the road is crooked or narrow. We don't worry about the van parked at the side of the road or the other obstacles along the way. We are simply trying to make momentary decisions and do the right thing in the right situation.[3]

The mistake many people make when seeking after wisdom is to assume that once it is found, it will enable them to see life from the control center. I have heard it described as "getting God's perspective on our world." I'm afraid many people think that means having a deep insight into the purpose of God in all the events of our lives, being able to discern why God has done what He has done in every situation and then knowing what He is planning to do next.

In reality, Packer's second illustration is closer to the true meaning of biblical wisdom. When we have acquired God's wisdom, we will be able to negotiate our lives through every situation, responding to the conditions of the road as God would want us to. It means that we will be clear-sighted and realistic - ruthlessly so - in looking at life as it is!

Such wisdom must have been characteristic of the early Christians. They were famous throughout the Roman Empire for the joy with which they met life's troubles. They suffered much and were persecuted. After life dictated that they would be disowned by their families and persecuted by their enemies, they suffered poverty, imprisonment and even martyrdom. However they were treated and no matter what life threw at them, their "wisdom" brought them joy. A remarkable testimony to their spirit is given in an ancient manuscript written by Aristedes, an Athenian philosopher of the second century:

> They observe scrupulously the commandment of their Messiah, they live honestly and soberly as the Lord their God commanded them. Every morning and at all times on account of the goodness of God toward them, they praise and laud Him and render thanks. If any righteous person of their number passes away from the world, they rejoice and give thanks to God. And when

a child is born to any of them, they praise God. And if it chances to die in its infancy, they praise God mightily as for one who passed through this world without sins.[4]

Such an outlook on life which is the fruit of wisdom seems to be a missing ingredient with many of us who call ourselves Christians. Even the small bumps in the road throw us off course and the sharp turns often cause us to stop dead in our tracks in fear. Because we cannot see to the end of the road, we are too paralyzed to move forward into the territory we can plainly view.

SEVEN PILLARS IN THE HOUSE OF WISDOM

Now that we have a working definition of wisdom, let's see if we can describe how it goes to work for us in our lives. Solomon provides the framework in Proverbs 9:1 where we read, "Wisdom is building her house and has hewn out her seven pillars upon which it may stand." Though this general statement is not meant to convey a seven-fold description of wisdom, I was struck by the coincidence of the *seven* synonyms for wisdom found in the first chapter of Proverbs. In some respects, they are like the colors in a rainbow. They all blend into one another, and yet any one of them could be used to represent the whole. There is great value in seeing them analyzed and compared.

1. Wisdom is Development - " A Skill"

"The Proverbs of Solomon, the Son of David,, the King of Israel, to know wisdom." The word for wisdom here is used thirty-seven times in the book of Proverbs. It is always used in the sense of a developed skill or mental ability. This wisdom is the capacity for skill or intellect that must be developed within an individual (Proverbs 9:9).

It is used in the Old Testament to describe the ability that God gave to Solomon for the express purpose of building the house of the Lord.

> Blessed be the Lord God of Israel, that made heaven and earth, who hath given to David the king a *wise* son, endued with prudence and understanding that he might build an house for the Lord and a house for His kingdom.   (2 Chronicles 2:12)

This same word describes the developed ability of Old Testament women who sewed Aaron's garments:

> And thou shalt speak unto all that are *wise-hearted*, whom I
> have filled with the spirit of wisdom that they may make Aaron's
> garments to consecrate him. (Exodus 28:3)

The word is used again to describe the ability of the craftsman in
Exodus 31:3:

> And I have filled him (Bezaliel) with the spirit of God, in
> wisdom, and in understanding, and in knowledge, and in all
> manner of workmanship. (Exodus 31:3)

2. Wisdom is Discipline - "Instruction"

This word is used some twenty-six times in the book of Proverbs.
It tells us by its use that wisdom will be hard to win. It is a quality
of character as well as a quality of the mind. The word has a note
of sternness and is sometimes translated as reproof or correction.
It teaches us that wisdom is not an extramural endeavor. Wisdom
is for disciples only.

Wisdom not only involves discipline. In some ways it *is* discipline
itself. Look with me at the first four verses of Proverbs chapter 2.
Here Solomon describes the discipline associated with the acquisition of wisdom. Note the words of intensity:

> My son, if thou wilt receive my words and hide my command-
> ments with thee, so that thou *incline thine ear* unto wisdom and
> *apply thine heart* unto understanding. Yea, if thou *criest after*
> knowledge and *lifteth up thy voice* for understanding. If thou
> *seekest* for her as silver and *searcheth* for her as for hid treasures.
> (Proverbs 2:1-4)

My sister, Dr. Maryalyce Jeremiah, is the women's basketball
coach at Indiana University in Bloomington, Indiana. Her opportunities include the privilege of listening to the philosophy of Bobby
Knight, the men's basketball coach at I.U. Not long ago, she told
me about an article in *Sports Illustrated* magazine that explained
some of Coach Knight's philosophy: "I would certainly not subscribe
to all of his ideas but his definition of discipline is one of the best
that I ever heard, and it's worth writing into your spiritual notebook.
*Discipline is doing what needs to be done, doing it when it needs
to be done, doing it the best it can be done, and doing it that way
every time you do it.*

I believe this is the thought behind Solomon's second word for
wisdom. Wisdom includes instruction that is locked into the

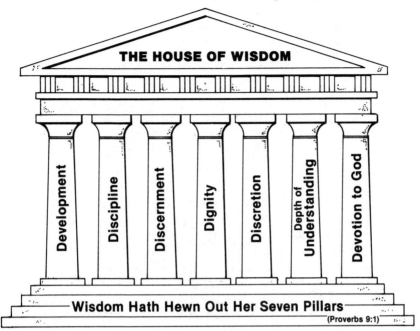

THE HOUSE OF WISDOM

Development | Discipline | Discernment | Dignity | Discretion | Depth of Understanding | Devotion to God

Wisdom Hath Hewn Out Her Seven Pillars

(Proverbs 9:1)

context of structure and discipline. Bible reading, Bible memory, Bible study, Bible meditation and prayer are all a part of the discipline necessary for true wisdom.

3. Wisdom is Discernment

The third word in Proverbs 1 is translated by an English phrase. Here it means "to perceive the words of understanding" (Proverbs 1:2). This same word is also used in chapter 2 and verse 7, "Apply thine heart unto understanding." It is best translated by our word "discernment."

It actually is the same root word from which we get the word "between." The word refers to the ability to make a decision between two options. Later in this book, we will take an in-depth look at the prayer of Solomon where he used this concept in talking to God, "Give to me an understanding heart that I might be able to discern between good and evil" (I Kings 3:9).

I think this is what Paul was asking God to give his Philippian friend:

> And this I pray that your love may abound yet more and more

> in knowledge and all judgment that you may approve the things
> that are excellent. (Philippians 1:9-10)

And the writer of Hebrews has this quality of wisdom in mind
when he writes:

> But solid food belongeth to them that are of full age, even those
> who by reason of use have their senses exercised to *discern* both
> good and evil. (Hebrews 5:14)

Five hundred years ago, our English word "understanding" didn't
mean exactly what it means today. In one of Shakespeare's writings,
ne of his characters says, "Why, to stand under, and to understand,
that's all the same." The word later came to mean "to see something
from the ground up." To understand then was to see something from
the ground up and to see all there was to see so as to get a clear
mental picture of the thing.

How desperately we need this aspect of wisdom; the ability to see
things clearly so that we will make proper choices and decisions.

One of my favorite stories is a supposedly true tale about an auto
manufacturer in Detroit, Michigan. Reportedly, they have a letter
on file that reads as follows:

> Dear Sir:
> I have one of your cars, and I have a complaint about it.
> My complaint is that it runs fine until I go out and buy vanilla
> ice cream. I know you think I'm crazy, but I'm serious. I buy
> my family ice cream every night. If I buy strawberry, chocolate
> or nut ice cream, my car starts fine, but if I buy vanilla ice
> cream, the dumb thing won't start.

Well, the top echelon in the company laughed about the letter but
dispatched a top-flight engineer to check the story. He went to the
car owner's house and was surprised to discover that he was a college graduate and that he lived in an affluent part of town.

Just as he had written, every night he would ask his family what
kind of ice cream they wanted and would head off toward the ice
cream store. True enough, the car started fine except when the man
bought vanilla ice cream and then it wouldn't start.

The engineer followed the man to the ice cream store for two full
weeks before he finally figured out the problem. In this particular
ice cream store, all of the flavored ice cream was in one section and
the vanilla ice cream was in another section. There was always a long

line of people waiting for the flavored ice cream, but there was never a line for the vanilla. When the car owner bought vanilla ice cream, he was only in the store for a few minutes, but when he bought flavored ice cream, he was in the store for at least ten minutes. The problem was not the flavor of the ice cream. The problem was time. Now the engineer could diagnose the problem.

The car had a vapor lock and every night that vapor lock went into action. The extra five or ten minutes it took to buy flavored ice cream gave the vapor lock time to disappear. But when he bought vanilla ice cream, he returned to the car immediately and the vapor lock kept the car from starting. Though it was true to say that the car wouldn't start when vanilla ice cream was purchased, discernment of the real problem was lacking. The owner didn't see the problem "from the ground up" and thus made some wrong assumptions.

Without the wisdom which God provides, we will be prone to similar mistakes.

4. Wisdom is Dignity

This word is found in verse 3, "to receive the instruction of wisdom." It is different from the first word translated in our Bibles as the word "wisdom." Its character shows in the verb form of the word which means to be successful . . . to do the right thing at the right time. It is always found in connection with three other words, "righteousness, judgment, and quality."

This unique aspect of wisdom might be defined by the word "circumspect." It is learning to behave with propriety and tact . . . as David did when Saul was having his jealous fits. Eve was thinking that she would have this kind of sophisticated wisdom when she took the forbidden fruit, but what she got was Satan's cheap substitute.

There is a little known Old Testament woman who wonderfully illustrates this characteristic of wisdom. Abigail's brief appearance is recorded for us in 1 Samuel 25.

The story begins with the account of Abigail's husband, Nabal. This wealthy man had three thousand sheep and one thousand goats. He lived in a place called Maon but his possessions were in Carmel. While Nabal's cattle were in Carmel, David and his men protected them from danger.

Now David and his men needed a favor from Nabal. Servants of David were dispatched to Nabal's home in Maon to request travel provisions and food. Nabal is described in 1 Samuel 25:3 as a "churlish man who was evil in all his doings." His response to David's request demonstrated that he was deserving of that reputation. Nabal said:

> Who is David? And who is the Son of Jesse? There be many servants nowadays that break every man from his master. Shall I then take my bread, and my water, and my flesh that I have killed for my shearers, and give it unto men, whom I know not whence they be? (1 Samuel 25:10-11)

When David's servants reported how Nabal had treated them, David was furious. "Get your swords and teach this Nabal a lesson." David and four hundred of his men marched toward Nabal's home to obliterate his name from the earth.

But wise Abigail, Nabal's wife, stepped into the picture. Her action, on behalf of her husband, presents a life-picture of this sixth characteristic of wisdom. As David and his men approached Nabal's home determined to destroy him, Abigail sent her servants out to meet them. They went equipped with two hundred loaves, two bottles of wine, five sheep ready-dressed, five measures of parched corn, one hundred clusters of raisins, and two hundred cakes of figs.

Abigail followed after her servants and when she saw David, fell down before him and begged him not to carry out his plan of destruction. "Please don't take my husband seriously," she said, "He is a worthless fellow. If I had been present when your servants came seeking help, I would have given them what they wanted." To make a long story short, David listened to Abigail and responded:

> Blessed be the Lord God of Israel, which sent thee this day to meet me. And blessed be thy advice, and blessed be thou, which hast kept me this day from coming to shed blood.
> (1 Samuel 25:33-34)

Abigail made such an impression on David by her cunning and wisdom that after Nabal died, David married her.

5. Wisdom is Discretion

"To give prudence to the sinful and to the young man knowledge and *discretion*." This word can be used in a bad sense as in Genesis 3:1 where the serpent is described as "subtle."

In the Book of Joshua, there is a story recorded of a man named Gibeon. I'm sure you remember how Gibeon and his men came to

Joshua camouflaged in old clothes, wearing shoes with holes in the bottom and carrying bags that appeared to be worn with use. They were afraid of Israel and determined to save their own lives by deceiving Joshua. They claimed to have come from a far distant country when in reality they were next-door neighbors. The Scripture says that Gibeon acted "wilily." The word literally means deceitfully, and it's the same word that is used in Proverbs for "discretion."

Proverbs 12:2 describes this kind of a person as a man of wicked devices. The evil connotation of discretion should not be found in a believer's life. The New Testament, however, speaks of godly discretion. We are instructed to be gentle as doves and wise as serpents. When it comes to evil, we are to be simple; but when it comes to good, we are to be wise.

6. Wisdom is Depth of Understanding

"A wise man will hear and increase learning and a man of understanding shall attain unto *wise counsels*." That's the sixth word for wisdom in our text. "Wise counsels" equals "depth of understanding." It means to know the workings behind something. The modern vernacular might phrase this word, "to know the ropes." This phrase is a nautical term and literally means to know the inner workings behind a matter.

I prayed for this aspect of wisdom when the Lord directed me to my present ministry. I had been in a church that I had started some twelve years before. I knew everything about that congregation. The structure, the leadership, and government had been my own creation. When I came to the Scott Memorial Baptist Church, it was a different story indeed.

When I attempted to explain to my friends back in the Midwest, the conversation went something like this:

"What's it like out there?"

"Well, we are one church with three different locations."

"What do you mean, three churches. Where are they?"

"Well, one's in the East, one's in the West, and one's in the North."

"How do you pastor a church in three locations?"

"Well, I preach in the East in the morning and in the West and the East at night and almost never at the North church."

"Isn't there a school there too?"

"Well, no, not exactly, there's a school system."

"A what?"

"A school system."

"You mean there's more than one school?"

"That's right! There are five elementary schools, two junior high schools and two high schools."

"What's this ICR thing I've been reading about?"

"Well, that's the Institute for Creation Research."

"How does that figure into the ministry?"

"Well, they don't have an official tie with the church, but they do have all of their offices in our Administration Building. In fact, my office is only a few doors from their lawyer's office."

"There's a lawyer in your Church Administration Building?"

"That's right! He works for the Institute for Creation Research and also does some work for our college."

"There's a college too?"

"Yes, Christian Heritage College has 435 students and they meet on the church campus!"

About this time, a puzzled expression would come across my friends' faces, and they would shrug their shoulders and change the subject. Their confusion was only a small matter compared to the utterly hopeless confusion I felt when I first came to Scott.

I spent two whole years learning the inner workings of Scott Memorial Church. It took me that long to "learn the ropes." I finally have some depth of understanding about my new assignment. I guess you would say I'm getting wiser.

7. Wisdom is Devotion to God

Though it is seventh in the list, it belongs first in terms of its importance. It surfaces first in Proverbs 1:7, "The fear of the Lord is the beginning of knowledge." This concept is also found elsewhere in the Scriptures. Here in Proverbs "the fear of the Lord" is a prominent truth.

> Fearing the Lord is a choice we make.   (Proverbs 1:29)
>
> The fear of the Lord can be understood.   (Proverbs 2:5)
>
> To fear the Lord is to hate evil, pride, arrogance, the evil way, and the froward mouth.   (Proverbs 8:13)
>
> The fear of the Lord prolongs our days upon the earth.
>   (Proverbs 10:27)

The fear of the Lord brings confidence.   (Proverbs 14:26)

The fear of the Lord is a fountain of life. (Proverbs 14:27)

The fear of the Lord is better than wealth. (Proverbs 15:16)

The fear of the Lord is instructional.   (Proverbs 15:33)

The fear of the Lord keeps one from evil.   (Proverbs 16:6)

The fear of the Lord brings satisfaction to life.(Proverbs 19:23)

The fear of the Lord is the secret of success.(Proverbs 22:4)

The fear of the Lord should become a lifestyle.(Proverbs 23:17)

The command is clear: "Fear the Lord" (Proverbs 3:7, 24:21). If you've ever asked a pastor or theology teacher what it means to "fear the Lord," you've probably heard something like this: "It doesn't mean to be afraid of, only to reverence or be in awe of." In the Union Prayer Manual, the word fear is replaced by the words "awe" and "reverence."

I'm not certain that we are justified in making such a quick transition from "fear" to "awe." I believe the "fear of the Lord" is an absolute requirement for attaining wisdom. I remember reading of one Puritan leader who said that he feared no man because he feared God so much.

We are told by some that to "fear God" is to denigrate the bond between God and man by moving the basis of the relationship from love to fear. Because we have believed this explanation, we have very slowly brought God to our level instead of exalting Him to His rightful place and worshipping Him in fear and reverence.

When Isaiah saw the Lord high and lifted up, he saw himself as a man of unclean lips and undone. It is only through the fear of God that we understand our total helplessness apart from Him. It is this sense of helplessness and emptiness that is the primary prerequisite for obtaining God's wisdom. (We'll say more about that in chapter 2.)

I believe this thought motivated David to pray this prayer recorded in Psalm 90:

> So teach us to number our days, that we may
> apply our hearts unto wisdom.

I heard of a businessman who took this prayer literally. Determining the importance of wisdom and the brevity of life, he made a

TEACH US TO NUMBER OUR DAYS

That We May Apply Our Hearts Unto Wisdom
Psalm 90

descending calendar to keep himself honest in his prayer. He determined the standard of living according to the Bible to be seventy years. He then multiplied 70 times 365 to arrive at the total number of days he might reasonably be expected to live. From that number he subtracted the number of days he had already lived and taking that total, made a descending calendar which he placed on his desk at the office, 5,430, 5,429, 5,428 . . . Each day he would remove the page for the day before, so that the total number of days he might reasonably expect to live would be visible.

How morbid, we say! Yet how challenging, numbering our days and applying our hearts to wisdom. When we realize how all-encompassing and life-changing this concept is, we will gladly live our lives in its pursuit.

These next chapters are intended to instruct, motivate, challenge and inspire us to that goal.

NOTES

1. Sprios Zodiatos, *The Behavior Of Belief* (Grand Rapids: Eerdmans, 1959), p. 163.
2. J. I. Packer, *Knowing God* (Downer's Grove: InterVarsity Press, 1973), p.92.
3. Ibid., p. 93.
4. Frank N. Magill, ed., "The Apology of Aristedes," in *Masterpieces of Christian Literature in Summary Form* (New York: Harper and Row, 1963), p. 12.

Four Keys To Wisdom

I heard about a frustrated mother whose two sons where driving her crazy. She had tried everything to keep them in line, when one day she had an over-the-fence discussion with a neighbor. "I took my son to our priest," reported her friend, "and he got him straightened out for good."

Because she had exhausted all of her options and didn't have a better idea, she followed her neighbor's advice and took her two sons to the local parish priest. The younger boy was left in the waiting room and the older boy was ushered into the solemn presence of the robe-clad clergyman.

Without so much as introducing himself, the priest stared into the eyes of the frightened boy and began his interrogation with this question: "Where is God?"

The boy was speechless. The priest spoke again, "Where is God?"

The young lad looked away, searching the room as if the answer might be found in the religious items that filled the office. He still did not answer. A little louder and with more emphasis, the priest asked for a third time, "Where is God?"

This time, the boy leaped to his feet and ran out of the office. When he came to the waiting room, he grabbed his brother by the hand and pulled him out the door. "Let's get out of here," he said, "They've lost God and they're trying to pin it on us."

If our understanding of wisdom is correct, then our problem is simple. Rediscover the presence of God in our lives, and we have found the straight path to the house of wisdom. But how do we do that? Where do we begin?

As I studied this question and read and reread the Word of God with this in mind, I began to see some consistent patterns. Our ability to acquire God's wisdom is not so much a matter of *doing* as it is of *being*. It isn't so much an *activity* as it is an *attitude*.

I once heard a preacher say that our attitude determines our altitude. When it comes to climbing the heights of God's wisdom, there is truth in that statement. Four basic attitudes are presented in the Bible as necessary prerequisites to the acquisition of wisdom.

Four Keys To The House of Wisdom

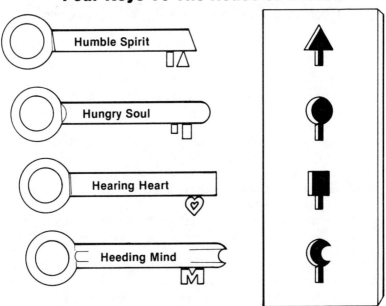

PREREQUISITE NUMBER ONE – A HUMBLE SPIRIT

The first step in acquiring wisdom is a proper understanding of one's relationship to God. The Psalmist says that "The fear of the Lord is the beginning of wisdom" (Psalm 111:10).

The son of the Psalmist put it this way:

> The fear of the Lord is the beginning of knowledge, but fools despise wisdom and instruction.   (Proverbs 1:7)

> The fear of the Lord is the beginning of wisdom, and the knowledge of the Holy One is understanding.(Proverbs 9:10)

> The fear of the Lord is the instruction of wisdom, and before honor is humility.   (Proverbs 15:33)

Job answered his own quest for wisdom with the same basic conclusion:

> Behold, the fear of the Lord, that is wisdom . . .(Job 28:28)

Charles Bridges asks the key question in his study of the Book of Proverbs:

> But what is the fear of the Lord? It is the affectionate reverence by which the child of God submits himself humbly and carefully to his Father's law. God's wrath is so bitter, and His love so sweet that there naturally arises a desire to please Him. And also—in view of falling short because of his own weakness and temptations—a holy watchfulness and fear, so "that I might not sin against thee." This enters into every area of life. The most mature pupil in God's school wants to be more completely molded by His teaching. The godly parent trains up his family under the Word's influence. The Christian scholar honors it as the beginning, the most important part of all his knowledge. He sees that it gives meaning and purpose to learning, and saves him from treacherous temptations that accompany knowledge.[1]

J. I. Packer explains how important this attitude is to the acquisition of wisdom:

> Not until we have become humble and teachable, standing in awe of God's holiness and sovereignty, acknowledging our own littleness, distrusting our own thoughts, and willing to have our minds turned upside down, can divine wisdom become ours. It is feared that many Christians spend all their lives in too unhumbled and conceited a frame of mind to ever gain wisdom from God at all.[2]

It is because of our bent toward independence and self-sufficiency that God warns us repeatedly against trusting our own judgment and wisdom:

> Be not wise in thine own eyes, fear the Lord and depart from evil. (Proverbs 3:7)

> Seest thou a man wise in his own conceits, there is more hope of a fool than in him. (Proverbs 26:12)

> Woe to them that are wise in their own eyes and prudent in their own sight. (Isaiah 5:21)

> Be not wise in your own conceit. (Romans 12:16)

My interest in the subject of God's wisdom came at a time when I was making a major change in my own life and ministry. After starting a church and pastoring it for some twelve years, I sensed God leading me to a new assignment.

Each week as I learned more about the challenge and responsibility of God's new calling in my life, I began to sense a growing feeling of despair. The words of Paul, "Who is sufficient for these things?" (2 Corinthians 2:16) described my attitude. You can imagine how encouraged I was to realize that my fear was merely a stepping stone to the help I needed from God.

James says that before we pray for wisdom, we must realize that we "lack" it (James 1:5). Jesus pronounced a special blessing on the poor in spirit (Matthew 5:3), and the wisest man who ever lived wrote that "with the lowly is wisdom" (Proverbs 11:2).

Over the gates of Plato's School, it was written, "Let no one who is not a geometrician enter." But over the door of wisdom's house is an invitation to the ignorant, the simple, the foolish, and young and the humble.

The prophet Jeremiah had it all together when he wrote:

> Let not the wise man glory in his wisdom, neither let the mighty man glory in his might, let not the rich man glory in his riches: But let him that glorieth glory in this, that he understandeth and knoweth me, that I am the Lord which exercise loving kindness, judgment, and righteousness in the earth: for in these things I delight, saith the Lord.
>
> (Jeremiah 9:23-24)

I am sure you have heard someone repeat this very interesting little paradigm:

> He that knows not and knows not that he knows not is a fool . . . shun him. He that knows not and knows that he knows not is simple . . . teach him. He that knows and knows not that he knows is asleep . . . wake him up. He that knows and knows that he knows is a wise man . . . follow him.

As time-honored as that statement is, it does not agree with the biblical concept of wisdom. A man who is wise according to God's definition knows too well his own weaknesses. He never assumes infallibility. He who knows most knows how little he knows.

William Cowper's beautiful lines comparing knowledge and wisdom conclude where the Bible does:

Knowledge and wisdom, far from being one,
Have ofttimes no connection, knowledge dwells In heads
    replete with thoughts of other men,
Wisdom in minds attentive to their own.
Knowledge a rude unprofitable mass,
The mere materials with which wisdom builds till
    smoothed and squared, and fitted to its place,
Does not encumber whom it seems to enrich.
Knowledge is proud that he has learned so much.
Wisdom is humble that he knows no more.[3]

PREREQUISITE NUMBER TWO—A HUNGRY SOUL

The second beatitude says it clearly, "Blessed are they who do hunger and thirst after righteousness for they shall be satisfied" (Matthew 5:6).

A. W. Tozer made much of the hunger factor. He wrote, "The great people of the Bible and Christian history have had an insatiable hunger for God. He wants to be wanted. Too bad that with many of us He waits so long, so very long in vain."[4]

When I read *The Spiritual Secrets of Hudson Taylor*, I remember copying his hunger statement in the flyleaf of my Bible. "I saw Him, and I sought Him, and I had Him, and I wanted Him."[5]

St. Augustine confessed his desire for God consistently. He wrote, "Who will give me what it takes to rest in you? Who will make it so you come into my heart and captivate it so I can forget my rottenness and take hold of you, the one good thing in my life."[6]

One thousand years later, Lady Julian of Norwich asked, "God, of your goodness give me yourself, for you are enough for me. If I ask anything less, I know I shall continue to want. Only in you I have everything."[7]

J. N. Darby put it stronger still:

> To be hungry is not enough. I must be really starving to know what is in His heart towards me. When the prodigal son was hungry, he went to feed upon the husks, but when he was starving, he turned to his father. To hunger and thirst really means to be desperate, to be starving, to feel life is ebbing out, to realize my urgent need to help.

They are all saying the same thing. *We have as much of God and His wisdom as we really want to have.* Our lack of wisdom is the result of our own lack of desire to know God.

Once again, this prerequisite is the clear and consistent teaching of God's Word.

> One thing have I desired of the Lord, that will I seek after: that I may dwell in the house of the Lord all the days of my life, to behold the beauty of the Lord, and to inquire in His temple.
> (Psalm 27:4)

> As the hart panteth after the waterbrook, so panteth my soul after thee, O God. My soul thirsteth for God, for the Living God.
> (Psalm 42:2-3)

> O God, thou art my God, early will I seek thee, my soul thirsteth for thee, my flesh longeth for thee in a dry and thirsty land, where no water is, to see thy power and glory as I have seen thee in the sanctuary.
> (Psalm 63:1-2)

> My soul breaketh for the longing that it hath unto thy judgments at all times.
> (Psalm 119:20)

> And ye shall seek for me, and find me, when ye shall search for me with all your whole heart.
> (Jeremiah 29:3)

The intensity of our longing after and hunger for God is captured in the Psalmist's term, "the whole heart." In Psalm 119 alone, we are instructed to "seek God with our whole heart" (v. 10), "Obtain God's Word with our whole heart" (v. 34), "Long after God's truth with our whole heart" (v. 40), "Entreat God's favor with our whole heart" (v. 58), "Keep God's precepts with our whole heart" (v. 69), "Cry unto God with our whole heart" (v. 145). If the opposite of whole-hearted seeking after God is half-hearted seeking after God, then for many of us, we know where our problem lies.

Tozer majored on the believer's hunger for God. In fact, he wrote a whole book on the subject entitled, *The Pursuit of God*. I quote a rather extensive passage from that book to drive home this truth in terms better than my own:

> Why do some people 'find' God in a way that others do not? Why does God manifest His presence to some and let multitudes of others struggle along in the halflight of imperfect Christian experience? Of course, the will of God is the same for all. He has no favorites with his household. All that He has ever done for any of His children, He will do for all of His children. The difference lies not with God but with us.
>
> Pick at random a score of great saints whose lives and

testimonies are widely known. Let them be Bible characters or well-known Christians of post-Biblical times. You will be struck instantly with the fact that the saints were not alike. Sometimes the unlikenesses were so great as to be positively glaring.

How different, for example, was Moses from Isaiah; how different was Elijah from David; how unlike each other were John and Paul, St. Francis and Luther, Finney and Thomas A. Kempis. The differences are as wide as human life itself; the differences of race, nationality, education, temperament, habit, and personal qualities. Yet, they walked, each in his day, upon a high road of spiritual living, far above the common way . . . Their differences must have been incidental and in the eyes of God of no significance. In some vital quality, they must have been alike. *What was it*?

I venture to suggest that the one vital quality which they had in common was spiritual receptivity. Something in them was open to heaven, something which urged them Godward. Without attempting anything like a profound analysis, I shall say simply that they had spiritual awareness and that they went on to cultivate it until it became the biggest thing in their lives.

They differed from the average person in that when they felt the inward longing, they did something about it . . . As David neatly put it, 'When thou sayest, seek ye my face; my heart said unto thee, they face, Lord, will I seek.'[8]

That's it, spiritual hunger! We have just about as much of God as we really want.

Before we examine the next prerequisite, however, let me take a moment to explain something I have learned about spiritual hunger. My teacher in this "course" has been Shirwood Wirt. In his book, *A Thirst For God*, he explains that physical and spiritual hunger, though alike in many ways, are very different fundamentally.[9]

For example, when we are hungry physically, we eat and we are satisfied. But when we are spiritually hungry, we eat and discover that our appetite for God and His Word is increased. That is why disiplined, consistent study of God's Word and regular participation in a Bible-teaching ministry is critical for the growth of our Christian lives.

But notice this! When we are physically hungry and we miss a meal, we are starved. Once again in the spiritual realm, it is just the opposite. When we begin to miss our spiritual meals, we begin to lose our appetites. That explains why Christians who neglect God's Word in their own personal lives find it easier and easier to neglect the public teaching and preaching of the Word of God in their local churches. Though we can't press it too far, our church attendance patterns may be saying much more about our spiritual lives than we would like to have made public!

The paradox of spiritual hunger is captured in one of St. Bernard's hymns:

> We taste Thee, O Living Bread,
> And long to feast upon Thee still
> We drink of Thee the Fountainhead
> And thirst our souls from Thee to fill.

PREREQUISITE NUMBER THREE – A HEARING HEART

We examined the prayer of Solomon in I Kings chapter 3. In his unique supplication to God, he asked for an understanding heart. The text literally says, "Give therefore thy servant a hearing heart. . . ." What a request! A hearing heart! If we have a humble spirit and a hungry soul, we must determine to be sensitive to what God may say to us through His Word and through His people as they share the principles of His Word.

Once again, the Proverbs extol the virtue of good listening:

A wise man will hear and will increase learning, and a man of understanding shall attain unto wise counsels: to understand a proverb, and the interpretation; the words of the wise, and their dark sayings. (Proberbs 1:5-6)

Give instruction to a wise man and he will be yet wiser; teach a just man and he will increase in learning. (Proverbs 9:9)

The way of a fool is right in his own eyes, but he that hearkeneth unto counsel is wise. (Proverbs 12:15)

The heart of the prudent getteth knowledge, and the ear of the wise seeketh knowledge. (Proverbs 18:15)

Hear counsel and receive instruction, that thou mayest be wise in thy latter end. (Proverbs 19:20)

The hearing ear and the seeing eye, the Lord hath made even both of them. (Proverbs 20:12)

When the wise is instructed, he receiveth knowledge.
(Proverbs 21:15)

Bow down thine ear and hear the words of the wise, and apply thine heart unto my knowledge. For it is a pleasant thing if thou keep them within thee; they shall withal be fitted in thy lips.
(Proverbs 22:17-18)

Hear thou, my son, and be wise, and guide thine heart in the way.   (Proverbs 23:19)

Recently, one of my favorite cartoon friends, Ziggy, was pictured passing a rather shabby character who was sitting on the sidewalk propped up against a building. Beside him was a sign that announced, "Good listener—25¢ for 5 minutes." Somehow I can't help but believe that Ziggy's friend had greatly undersold his services. In our communication-conscious world, we are suffering from a terrible shortage of good listeners.

You may have heard the story of the little boy who was riding a bus with his father. His nose was pressed against the glass. He kept asking his Dad questions. "What's on that truck, Daddy?"

"I don't know," mumbled his father, immersed in the newspaper.

"Where does the rain come from?"

"Don't bother me."

"What does that sign say?"

"Quit pestering me."

A passenger riding behind the father, tapped him on the shoulder, and he said, "Curious little boy you have there."

"Sure," said the father, "How else is he going to learn?"

That's the way we listen, isn't it! There is so much of God's wisdom all around us, available to us from those who have walked with God before us, but we have to be willing to listen.

Almost every day, the classified section of our paper advertises courses and seminars guaranteed to make us better speakers. But, where are the courses designed to make us better listeners?

We give our graduates awards for good speaking, but I have never seen an award for excellent listening. Anatomically speaking, we are constructed to devote more time to listening than speaking. God gave us two ears and one mouth. Yet, for most of us, the mouth is surely overworked, and the ears are in a state of semi-retirement. One man explained it this way, "A wise man talks because he has something to say. Fools talk because they have to say something."

Recently, I read of a bartender who was training a young apprentice. He saw the novice hard at work trying to be witty and humorous with the customers. Unfortunately, the apprentice wasn't making much of an impression. The veteran called the young man over and gave him the distilled wisdom of his years of experience. "Listen, kid, listen. Don't talk. These guys want to talk. If they wanted to listen, they would go home."

Bridges reminds us that:

> Hearing is a great medium of knowledge, Moses was instructed by Jethro (Exodus 18:17-26); the disciples by our Lord (Matthew 13:11-16; John 16:12); the apostles by Peter (Acts 11:2-18); Apollos was instructed by Priscilla and Aquila in the way of God more accurately" (Acts 18:24-26). We gather knowledge when we listen; we spend it when we teach; but if we spend; before we gather, we'll soon be bankrupt. The longer we learn, the more we feel that we are learners, and the more willing we are to listen, the more we believe we can learn.[10]

PREREQUISITE NUMBER FOUR – A HEEDING MIND

A humble spirit . . . I need God. *A hungry soul* . . . I must have God. *A hearing heart* . . . I will listen to God's voice and finally, *a heeding mind* . . . I will obey God.

To know that we need Him is important! To reach out for Him is imperative. To hear what He has to say is crucial. But, it is all meaningless if we have not determined to do what He tells us.

Whoso *keepeth* the law is a wise son (Proverbs 28:7).

There is a very unusual passage of Scripture which *nationalizes* this principle. It is found in the Old Testament Book of Deuteronomy:

> Behold, I have taught you statutes and judgments, even as the Lord my God commanded me, that ye should do so in the land whither ye go to possess it.   (Deuteronomy 4:5)

Now listen to this:

> Keep therefore and do them; *for this is your wisdom* and your understanding in the sight of the nations, which shall hear all these statutes and say, Surely this great nation is a wise and understanding people.   (Deuteronomy 4:6)

Moses' words to his people are valid for today. We are not wise because we *have* God's Word. . . .We are not wise because we *desire* God's Word. . . .We are not even wise because we *read* God's Word. We are wise only when we keep and *obey* God's Word.

God's Word is not ours for the purpose of *possible* adherence. It is ours to obey. In fact, that is really the *only* reason God gave it to us. It is not a book that we study so that we might gather information about divine truths. We are not committed to God's Word so that we might be experts in the cultural living of another generation. God gave us this Book, the Bible, so that we might know what to do and what not to do.

The timeless principles embodied in this revelation from the Father are to be followed today even as they were during the time when the revelation was being given by God.

After the death of Moses, God spoke directly to Joshua, his successor, and explained exactly what it would take for him to be as prosperous and successful as Moses. His words are preserved for us in Joshua 1. It is the only passage I know in the Bible that uses the words "success" and "prosperity" in connection with the Christian experience.

The Master Key to Wisdom

Read It Obediently

Follow It Exclusively

Believe It Totally

God's Word

Study It Continually

Only be thou strong and very courageous, that thou mayest observe to do according to all the law, which Moses my servant commanded thee; turn not from it to the right hand or to the left, that thou mayest prosper withersoever thou goest.

> This book of the law shall not depart out of thy mouth, but
> thou shalt meditate therein day and night, that thou mayest
> observe to do according to all that is written therein; for then
> thou shalt make thy way prosperous, and then thou shalt have
> good success. (Joshua 1:7-8)

God says that the key to success and prosperity is the Word of
God . . . the law . . . the Bible. Joshua was to:

Read it obediently. Two times the Lord used this expression,
"Observe to do." In other words, Joshua was to read it for the sole
purpose of obeying it!

Follow it exclusively. The book of the law was not to be one among
many sources considered. It was not to be mixed together with other
information and then followed. It was to be followed exclusively.
"Turn not from it to the right hand or to the left."

Believe it totally. Joshua was not permitted the option to choose
what sections of God's Word he would believe and what sections
he would ignore. He was to "observe to do according to all that
is written therein" (v. 8). He was to follow "all the law" (v. 7).

Study it continually. God told Joshua "to meditate in the law day
and night" (v. 7).

The Lord told Joshua that by following these instructions he would
insure prosperity and success in his life and leadership. God's promise
is not bound by time. It is His promise to us today. When we believe
God's Word and obey it, we guarantee God's blessing upon our lives
. . . that is success . . . that is prosperity . . . that is wisdom!

Several years ago, I was invited to speak in a church in West
Virginia. One of the members of that congregation took me on a
tour of one of the coal mines in that area. Before being lowered into
the mine shaft, he gave me one of the carbide lamps that miners
wear as a part of their headgear.

After we were deep in the mine shaft, he signaled to the surface
control center and all the lights in the shaft were turned off. I have
never been in such darkness in my life. The only source of light was
the small lamp I was wearing. I remember being afraid to move at
first. I could not see ahead or even to the side.

But I discovered something quickly! As soon as I walked into the
light that I had, the light was projected an additional step into the
darkness. As long as I walked in the beam I had, there was always
enough light on my pathway to keep me from stumbling and to
guarantee my progress.

On many occasions, I have seen the application of this experience to my own spiritual journey. I don't have all of the answers for the rest of my life. I do not have the wisdom I need from God for next week's problems. But as I read God's Word for today, there is wisdom for my present needs. I have God's promise that as I walk in the light God has given me now, I need not fear a day of darkness!

NOTES

1. Charles Bridges, *A Modern Study In The Book of Proverbs* (Mott Media, Milford, MI, 1978), p. 4.

2. J. I. Packer, *Knowing God* (Downers Grove: InterVarsity Press, 1973), pp. 90-91.

3. William Cowper, "The Task," in *Masterpieces of Religious Verse*), ed. James D. Morrison (New York: Harper and Brother Pub., 1948), p. 397.

4. A. W. Tozer, *The Pursuit of God* (Harrisburg: Christian Pub. Co., 1948), p. 17.

5. Howard Taylor, *Hudson Taylor's Spiritual Secret* (Chicago: Moody Press, 1979), p. 21.

6. Sherwood E. Wirt, trans., *The Confessions of Augustine In Modern English* (Grand Rapids: Zondervan Pub., 1977), p. 4.

7. Lady Julian of Norwish, *Revelations of Divine Love* (London: Methuen, 1911), p. 12.

8. A. W. Tozer, *The Pursuit Of God*, pp. 66-67.

9. Sherwood E. Wirt, *A Thirst For God* (Grand Rapids: Zondervan Pub., 1980), p. 25.

10. Charles Bridges, *A Modern Study in the Book of Proverbs*, p. 3.

3

The Wisdom Of The World

A young minister was called to pastor a very influential church in a college town. As he stood to preach for the first time and looked out over his audience, he was embarrassed by the thought of criticism in his cultivated congregation.

He sought counsel from his father, an old and wise pastor. He said, "Dad, I'm hampered in my ministry and in the church I'm now serving. For if I cite anything from geology, there is professor "A", teacher of that science, and he is right before me. And if I use an illustration from Roman mythology, there is professor "B" ready to trip me up for any little inaccuracy. If I choose something in English literature that pleases me, I am cowarded by the presence of the learned man who teaches that course. What in the world can I do?"

The sagacious old man replied, "Son, don't be discouraged. Preach the gospel. They probably won't know very much about that at all."

His father was right in line with the apostle Paul. "Not many wise are chosen!" (1 Corinthians 1:26). The world by its wisdom cannot know God. No man has educated himself into the kingdom of God, for the wisdom of God and wisdom of man are diametrically opposed to each other.

In these next two chapters we're going to look at the contrast that is presented by James . . . the contrast of the wisdom of the Word and the wisdom of the world. Only one letter distinguishes the "Word" from the "world" but the difference between the two philosophies is eternal in scope.

James describes the wisdom of this age in the third chapter of his epistle. He begins with a question:

> Who is a wise man and endued with knowledge among you? Let him show out of a good conversation his works with meekness of wisdom. But if ye have bitter envying and strife in your hearts, glory not, and lie not against the truth. This wisdom descendeth not from above, but is earthly, sensual, devilish. For where envying and strife is, there is confusion and every evil work. (James 3:13-16)

As we unfold this key passage of Scripture, we will do it logically instead of chronologically. Let's notice first the origin of world's wisdom.

THE ORIGIN OF THE WORLD'S WISDOM

This wisdom descendeth not from above, but is earthly, sensual, demonical . . . (James 3:15).

The simple but startling truth is this: the world's wisdom does not keep coming down from above. The phrase "descendeth not" is a participle and it describes a continuous action. As we shall learn, God's wisdom keeps coming down from above in daily dosages, but the wisdom of the world has no connection with heaven whatsoever.

James says that the wisdom of the world finds its source in three areas. First of all, he describes it as "earthly." Paul calls this the wisdom of the world.

Earthly Wisdom

> Where is the wise? Where is the scribe? Where is the disputer of this world? Hath not God made foolish the wisdom of this world? For after that, in the wisdom of God, the world by wisdom knew not God, it pleased God by the foolishness of preaching to save them that believe. (1 Corinthians 1:20, 21)

Paul teaches us in 1 Corinthians that the wisdom of the world is in total contrast to the wisdom of God. Note the differences:

> The world's wisdom is the wisdom of words. (1 Corinthians 1:17-2:4)
> God's wisdom is the wisdom of power. (1 Corinthians 2:4-5)

THE WISDOM OF THE WORLD

OUTCOME

Confusion

Every Evil Work

OPERATION

Outright Deceit

Arrogant Boasting

ORIGIN

Earthly
Sensual
Satanic

Selfish
Ambition

Bitter
Envying

The world's wisdom operates by man's word.(1 Corinthians 2:4)
God's wisdom operates by the Spirit's words.
(1 Corinthians 2:13)

The world's wisdom is championed by the spirit of the world.
(1 Corinthians 2:12)
God's wisdom is championed by the Spirit of God.
(1 Corinthians 2:12)

The world's wisdom is foolishness to God.(1 Corinthians 1:20)
God's wisdom is foolishness to the world.(1 Corinthians 2:14)

The world's wisdom is declared by the philosopher.
(1 Corinthians 1:20)
God's wisdom is declared by the preacher.
(1 Corinthians 2:4; 1:21)

The world's wisdom brings ignorance. (1 Corinthians 1:21)
God's wisdom brings knowledge.   (1 Corinthians 2:12)

The world's wisdom leads to condemnation.(1 Corinthians 1:18)
God's wisdom leads to salvation.   (1 Corinthians 1:18, 2:7)

From the beginning of time, man has been trying to get to God
by his own wisdom but it has never worked. In fact, it has backfired
on man as Paul explains in Romans:

> Because that when they knew God, they glorified him not as
> God, neither were thankful; but became vain in their imagina-
> tions, and their foolish heart was darkened. Professing
> themselves to be wise, they become fools. (Romans 1:21-22)

Even Christians must fight the temptation to revert to the world's
wisdom in their Christian experience. Paul warned the Colossians
against this:

> Beware lest any man spoil you through philosophy and vain
> deceit, after the tradition of men, after the *rudiments of the
> world*, and not after Christ.   (Colossians 2:8)

Whenever man has tried to govern his life by the wisdom of the
world, he has ended up defeated, discouraged, and disappointed.
Think back to the beginning of biblical history and note the consistent pattern of failure:

(1) The Tower of Babel was man's attempt to reach God through
his own wisdom. The result was total confusion.

TWO KINDS OF WISDOM IN I CORINTHIANS

THE WORLD'S WISDOM	GOD'S WISDOM
Wisdom of Words - 1:17-2:4	Wisdom of Power - 2:4-5
By Man's Word - 2:4	By Spirit's Words - 2:13
Spirit of the World - 2:12	Spirit of God - 2:12
Foolishness to God - 1:20	Foolishness to the World - 2:14
Philosopher - 1:20	Preacher - 2:4, 1:21
Brings Ignorance - 1:21	Brings Knowledge - 2:12
Leads to Condemnation - 1:18	Leads to Salvation - 1:18, 2:7

(2) Abraham followed the wisdom of the world when he left God's appointed place during a time of famine. It made sense to go to Egypt but the result for Abraham was his sinful relationship with Hagar and ultimately the birth of Ishmael. The fallout from that decision is felt even today as the tension in the Middle East continues to rise.

(3) Lot followed the wisdom of the world and chose all the good land. His choice made sense on paper but the result was Lot's spiritual demise and the loss of his family.

We could go on through the pages of the Old and New Testaments and cite example after example of the world's wisdom and its evil effects. Instead of going forward in the Scripture, however, I want you to join me as we turn backward to the very beginning of the Bible; backward to the story of the beautiful Garden of Eden, the birthplace of man's wisdom.

The story of man's fall, recorded in Genesis chapter 3, provides the first mention of the world's wisdom. Here are the words of Satan the tempter as he promises Eve this new kind of wisdom and here is her response as she embraces his promise of a new kind of wisdom which she had not known before:

> And the serpent said unto the woman, Ye shall not surely die: for God doth know that in the day ye eat thereof, then your eyes shall be opened, and ye shall be as God, knowing good and evil. And when the woman saw that the tree was good for food, and that it was pleasant to the eyes, and a tree to be desired *to make one wise*, she took of the fruit and did eat, and gave also unto her husband with her; and he did eat.(Genesis 3:4-6)

The wisdom Adam and Eve received when they disobeyed God in favor of Satan's promise was the wisdom of the world which James says is "earthly", sensual, and demonical.

Sensual Wisdom of the World

The word sensual is the Greek word "pseuke." It is a word which means "natural" or "soulish." It is the word which is translated in 1 Corinthians 2:14 as "the natural man." It is also given that same translation in 1 Corinthians 15:44 and 46. Interestingly enough, the words *psy*chology and *psy*chiatry are derivitives of the Greek word for "natural."

When this word is used here to describe the wisdom of the world, it speaks of this wisdom as being "natural" as opposed to "spiritual." In the contexts of both of the above passages in 1 Corinthians, the word "natural" is used in direct contrast to the word "spiritual."

Dr. James Boyer says there are four things which are always true of the natural man:

(1) He has a limited nature. His spirit is dead and therefore he cannot respond to God.

(2) He has a prejudiced disposition. The things of God are not welcomed in his life.

(3) He has a distorted judgment. The things of God are moronic to him.

(4) He has inadequate abilities. He lacks the necessary equipment to examine spiritual things. He is like a blind man in an art gallery . . . like a deaf man at a symphony.

It's like little Petunia who had a stomachache and was telling her mother how badly she felt. In reply mother said, "Honey, that's because your tummy is empty." That evening at church the pastor remarked that he had a splitting headache. Petunia leaned over and said to her mother, "That's because his head is empty, he'd feel better if he had something in it."

The inadequacy of the world's wisdom is summarized by the word "natural." Man by his own natural wisdom is limited in his quest for God. He has no adequate equipment in his being to relate to God.

The wisdom of the world is of the earth, earthly; and of the flesh, fleshly, but note also that it is of the devil, devilish.

Satanic Wisdom

When the word "demonical" is used to describe the world's wisdom, it settles once and for all the identity of the mastermind behind this world's wisdom. It is Satan himself.

The wisdom of Satan is illustrated graphically by something Paul Harvey said on one of his coast to coast broadcasts. He called his talk, "If I Were The Devil."

> If I were the Prince of Darkness, I would want to engulf the whole world in darkness. I'd have a third of the world's real estate and four-fifths of its population already. But I would not be happy until I seized the ripest apple on the tree, so I would set about, however necessary, to take over the United States.

I would begin with a campaign of whispers. With the wisdom of a serpent I would whisper, "The Bible is a myth." I would convince them that man created God, instead of the other way. I'd whisper that what is bad is good and what is good is square.

In the ears of the young married, I'd whisper that work is debasing, cocktail parties are good for you. I'd caution them not to be extreme in religion, patriotism, or in moral conduct.

And to the old, I would teach them to pray after me, "Our Father which art in Washington."

Then I'd get organized. I'd educate authors on how to make lurid literature exciting so that everything else would appear dull and uninteresting. I'd threaten TV with dirtier movies and vice versa. I'd peddle narcotics to whoever I could. I'd sell alcohol to ladies and gentlemen of distinction. I'd tranquilize all the rest with pills.

If I were the devil, I would encourage schools to refine young intellects but to neglect to discipline their emotions and I would let them run wild.

I'd designate an atheist to front for me in the highest courts of the land and I'd get preachers to say, "It's all right."

I'd infiltrate the unions and I'd urge more loafing and less working. Idle hands always have worked well for me.

With flattery and the promise of power, I would get the courts to vote against God and in favor of pornography. I would evict God from all the courthouses and from the schoolhouses and then from the house of Congress.

Then in His own churches, I'd substitute psychology for religion and I would deify science.

If I were Satan, I would make the symbol of Easter an egg, and the symbol of Christmas, a bottle.

If I were the devil, I would take from those who have and give to those who wanted until I had killed the incentive for all ambition. Then by police stat, I would force everybody back to work.

If I were Satan, I'd just keep on doing what I'm doing; and the whole world would go to hell, as sure as the devil."[2]

Satan's wisdom is alive and well, and you and I are more affected by it than we know. It is the dominating influence in our world. It is piped into our homes on the average of six hours per day and without constant vigil, we are conformed by its principles into the world's image.

The wisdom of the world is of the earth, earthly, of the flesh, fleshly, and of the devil, devilish. John the apostle summarized this three-fold attack upon the Christian in 1 John 2:15-17:

> Love not the world, neither the things that are in the world.
> If any man love the world, the love of the Father is not in him.
> For all that is in the world, the lust of the flesh, and the lust
> of the eyes, and the pride of life, is not of the Father, but is
> of the world. And the world passeth away and the lust thereof:
> but he that doeth the will of God abideth forever.

The wisdom of the world operates through "the lust of the flesh, the lust of the eyes, and the pride of life." It was this three-fold attack that Satan used on Eve (Genesis 3:1-7). It was the same strategy he tried to implement when he tempted Jesus Christ (Matthew 4:1-11). And it is still his battle plan for you and for me today.

The crucial thing to keep in mind, if you are a believer, is this: the wisdom of the world belongs to the old life, the life BC, before Christ. It is not to characterize the new you. You are to live in a new realm. That's what Paul was trying to get across to the Ephesian believers when he wrote these words:

> And you hath he made alive, who were dead in tresspasses and
> sins; In which times ye walked *according to the course of this*
> *world, according to the Prince of the power of the air*, the spirit
> that now worketh in the sons of disobedience; among whom
> also we all had our manner of life in times past in *the lusts of*
> *the flesh*, and of the mind, and were by nature the children of
> wrath, even as others, but God who is rich in mercy . . . hath
> made us alive together with Christ.   (Ephesians 2:1-5)

THE OPERATION OF THE WORLD'S WISDOM

James presents four distinct characteristics of the world's wisdom. This is how the world's wisdom operates:

Bitter Envying

The wisdom of the world exalts man and tries to glorify him. The person who operates on the basis of the world's wisdom is always seeking to promote himself. It is reminiscent of the argument among the apostles over the place of honor in the kingdom. The number one ploy of such a person is the age-old game of pushing one's self up by pushing someone else down.

The word "bitter" here is the New Testament word for the verb "to cut." Literally it means to be filled with cutting jealousy, or as we say it in our day, to cut others down.

The secular booksellers are not even trying to cover up their philosophy anymore. They've gone public! Books on how to be number one . . . how to intimidate your opponent . . . your employees . . . your wife . . . or your date, are now hitting the best-sellers list. It's the world's wisdom, packaged and ready to market and people are not only buying the books, they are also buying into the philosophy.

Selfish Ambition

The word "strife" is the translation we read in most of our Bibles. This word was used in New Testament times to describe a politician who was canvassing for his job. Later the word came to mean "a party spirit." Today we would call such a person "a manipulator."

If any one aspect of the world's wisdom takes precedence over the others in the church today, it is certainly this concept of manipulation. We manipulate to get our man in office. We manipulate to get ourselves elected. We try to befriend influential people so we can manipulate others through them. In opposition to the wisdom of God which is pure and peaceable, this wisdom of the world has a hidden agenda. Don't forget, such practices find their source in Satan.

Barclay reminds us that:

> You can tell what a man's relationship with God is by looking at his relationship with other people. If a man is at variance with fellow man and if he's a quarrelsome, competitive, argumentative trouble-making creature, he may be a diligent church-attender, he may even be a church office-bearer, but he's not a man of God. If a man is distant from his fellow man, it is good proof that he is distant from God. If he is divided from his fellow man, he is divided from God.[3]

Paul settles this issue for Christians everywhere when he writes, "Let *nothing* be done through strife or vainglory, but in lowliness of mind let each esteem others better than themselves" (Philippians 2:3).

Arrogant Boasting

The phrase "glory not" is a warning against arrogance and bragging. The wisdom of the world is identified by the arrogance of the one who is under its spell. Pride loves to boast.

Paul was dealing with this as he wrote the second letter to the Corinthians. He wrote that letter because he was being constantly attacked by the Corinthian people. In this moving passage of his letter, he explains why some people boast and he points out why it is such an absurd thing to do:

> For we dare not make ourselves of the number, or compare ourselves with some that commend themselves; but they, measuring themselves by themselves, and comparing themselves among themselves, are not wise.   (2 Corinthians 10:12)

According to Paul, such boasting is unwise because it is based on the absurdity of self-comparison. The whole concept makes me think of a prayer that was jokingly written by one of the ladies in our church after she heard me preach on the problem of pride. The poem drips with sarcasm, but it is not far from the attitude which James describes:

> I thank you, Lord, for giving me terrific looks, a brilliant mind, and sparkling personality that's spiritually inclined.

> I love my kids and Christian mate, our friendly church and Sunday school, our ranch-style home with patio and solar-heated swimming pool.

> I know my talents come from you; I'm praised for my angelic voice that sings and teaches weaker ones the way to make a godly choice.

> And thanks for my prestigious job and giving me an added gift— that anything my pen jots down becomes indeed, inspired script.

> You ought to bless every Christian; some lives seem ready to

crumble, but I am proud that you blessed me— I guess it's because I'm so humble.

Outright Deceit

"Lie not against the truth"—Now watch closely how all of these characteristics fit together. When one has selfish ambition, that leads to a party spirit or an attempt to elevate one's self. In order to be elevated, arrogant boasting must be utilized. Arrogant boasting inevitably leads to outright deceit . . . lying.

Unfortunately, one of the easiest places to view the wisdom of the world in operation is at the next pastors' conference you attend. Pastors, young and old, attempting to elevate themselves in the eyes of their peers, often resort to the world's methods.

You may have heard the story of the Baptist preacher and his Sunday school superintendent who were marooned on a totally uninhabited island. Though they were sure that they were all alone on the island, they decided on Saturday night that they should have a Sunday school workers' meeting to plan for Sunday school the next day. As they met to discuss the next day's services, they followed their usual practice of setting a goal. For attendance, their goal was four people.

The next day they counted their Sunday school attendance and sure enough, there were five in attendance, which proves one of two things. Either Baptists can find people where there are none, or they lie about their statistics.

One pastor, who was trying to elevate himself in the eyes of his ministerial friends, was known to exaggerate his statistics. One day he was confronted about his dishonesty and he replied with this bit of reasoning: "If I lie about my statistics, and you know that I lie about my statistics, and I know that you know that I lie about my statistics, isn't that like telling the truth?"

No, that's not like telling the truth . . . that's lying! But it is the certain result of trying to justify ourselves by our own standards and it belongs totally to the world's philosophy.

THE OUTCOME OF THE WORLD'S WISDOM

"For where envying and strife are, there is confusion and every evil work" (James 3:16).

The two consequences of the world's wisdom are clearly marked out for us . . . "confusion and every evil work."

Confusion

The word confusion means "to disturb." It is sometimes used to describe anarchy. Let's look at the two occasions where the word is used in the Book of James:

James 1:8—"A double-minded man is unstable in all his ways."

The word "unstable" is the same word as the word "confusion" in the text we are studying.

James 3:8—"But the tongue can no man tame; it is an unruly evil, full of deadly poison."

The word "unruly" is the same word as the word "confusion" in our text.

Wherever the wisdom of the world operates, the result is instability, chaos, and convulsive conditions.

When you think about this for a moment, you suddenly realize why it is such a struggle for Christians to function in the work force of the world. Confusion is the best the world has to offer.

Every Evil Work

The word "evil" here does not mean "bad"; it literally means "worthless," "good-for-nothing." The wisdom of the world comes to nothing; it is without any value. Isaiah, the prophet, spoke of the wisdom of the wise men as "perishing" (Isaiah 29:14).

An infidel once bequeathed his farm to the devil. The will was studied by the courts and it was decided that the only way they could carry out such a will was to order that the farm be left untouched by human hands throughout its entire history. In a few years, it had grown up in brush and weeds, the buildings tumbled down, and the whole picture presented a scene of desolation and ugliness. That's what happens to anything that is left to Satan and his world.

It is the proverbial story of the man who spends all of his life trying to climb the ladder of success, and when he gets to the top, he discovers it is leaning against the wrong wall.

William Barclay summarizes this whole passage when he writes:

James describes this arrogant and bitter wisdom in its effects. The most notable thing about it is this, that it issues in this order. That is to say, instead of bringing people together, it drives them apart. Instead of producing peace, it produces strife. Instead of producing a fellowship, it produces a disruption in personal relationships. There is a kind of person who is undoubtedly clever. He has an acute brain and a skillful tongue. But his effect in any committee, in any church, in any group, is to cause trouble, to drive people apart, to foment strife, to disturb personal relationships. It is a sobering thing to remember that what that man possesses is devilish rather than divine. And that such a man is engaged in Satan's work and not in God's work.[4]

Paul feared that this was the kind of wisdom that was operating in Corinth, and when he wrote his second letter to them, he said so:

> For I fear lest, when I come, I shall not find you such as I would, and that I shall be found unto you such as ye would not; lest there be debates, envyings, wraths, strifes, backbitings, whisperings, conceit, disorders. (2 Corinthians 12:20)

John, the apostle, described another church where such wisdom was operative when he wrote his letter to the Church of Laodicea:

> So, then, because thou art lukewarm, and neither cold nor hot, I will spew thee out of my mouth.
> Because thou sayest, I am rich, and increased with goods, and have need of nothing, and knowest not that thou art wretched, and miserable, and poor, and blind, and naked.
> (Revelation 3:16-17)

There is a better wisdom, a better word, and a better way. It is in contrast to all that we have studied in this chapter. It is the wisdom of God and is the theme for our next discussion.

NOTES

1. Roy R. Roberts, *Life In The Pressure Cooker* (Winona Lake: *BMH Books* 1977), p. 93.

2. Paul Harvey, "If I Were The Devil," *Moody Monthly* 67 (July/August 1967): 25.

3. William Barclay, *The Letters of James and Peter* (Philadelphia: Westminister Press, 1977), p. 94.

4. Ibid.

4

Wisdom From Above

At the Rockefeller Center in New York City, there are four large murals that hang on the wall. The first painting is of a primitive man laboring with his hands, attempting to survive his alien environment. Next to this painting is the portrayal of man having become the creator of tools, and the comforts of civilization have been multiplied. The third mural shows man to be both master and servant of the machine. The vast forces of the material world are now under his direction and his control. Our eyes move to the last painting with a sense of overwhelming surprise. It seems so out of context with the other three. Jesus Christ is the theme of this presentation, and He is seen in the setting of His Sermon on the Mount. Struggling up to Him are masses of men and women and children. Underneath that fourth mural, the mural of Christ, are inscribed these words:

> Man's ultimate destiny depends not on whether he can learn new lessons or make new discoveries or conquests but on his acceptance of the lesson that was taught him over two thousand years ago.[1]

This is the artist's way of saying that true wisdom for man is dependent upon man's ability to adjust to and accept God's revealed truth. This wisdom is man, as the creature, in proper perspective to God, the Creator.

When James asks, "Who is a wise man and endued with wisdom," he is asking a very important question. He answers his own question by saying that such a man shows by his life that he has a right relationship with God.

The pseudo-wisdom which we studied in the last chapter comes from the world and is worldly. It comes from the flesh and is fleshly.

It comes from the devil and is devilish. This pseudo-wisdom is devisively envious, selfishly ambitious, arrogantly boastful, and outwardly deceitful. The product of this imitation of God's wisdom is confusion and every evil work. A man who chooses the world's wisdom over God's wisdom will spend his life in futility and frustration.

James now presents an alternative. He gives us an option that will keep us from the pitfalls of man's wisdom. It is an option that protects the body of Christ, which is the church, from the dissension and strife which marks so many modern day assemblies.

Guy King in his commentary on this passage warns that:

> When Mr. Worldly-wise is allowed to be in the church, the tide of spiritual revival has been stayed. The holy task of soul-winning has been impaired. The commanding voice of Christian testimony has been silenced. And the growing experience of blessed intimacy with God has been arrested. Yes, and many more deplorable effects have ensued when worldly-wisdom has been allowed to have its way.[2]

Someone has given this truth a modern expression with these words: "The man who is wise in his own eyes is about to give his church a good case of vapor lock."

As we look at the real wisdom that comes from above, we must see it against the backdrop of the wisdom from below.

THE SOURCE OF HEAVENLY WISDOM

"This wisdom . . . is from above" (James 3:17). James uses a present tense participle to make his point. He says, "Wisdom *is coming* from above. Wisdom from above is not available in one-time allotments, nor is it to be procured on the installment plan. James presents it as a steady flow from the mind of God to His children. It just keeps on coming. The supply of God's wisdom never runs dry. It comes to us continually from above to meet the demands of each hour.

The Jews have an old tradition that when they were being fed in the wilderness by the manna from heaven, what they received was indicative of how they lived. If a man lived by the law, according to the tradition, his manna every morning would be whatever food he wanted it to be. What the Israelite received from God was just what he needed for the day.

The tradition of the Jews is nothing more than that—just a tradition, but it illustrates a truth about the nature of God's wisdom. When we walk with Him in the light of His Word, He daily gives us the wisdom we need for our lives.

In James 1:5, we are taught that wisdom comes from God in response to our prayer. We will devote an entire chapter to the explanation of this verse:

> If any of you lack wisdom, let him ask of God that giveth to all men liberally and upbraideth not; and it shall be given him.
>
> (James 1:5)

The seventeenth verse of that chapter further amplifies that by reminding us that:

> Every good gift and every perfect gift is from above, and cometh down from the Father of Lights with whom is no variableness, neither shadow of turning.   (James 1:17)

Our wisdom originates with God and comes from above, just as our citizenship is in heaven:

> For our conversation is in heaven; from whence also we look for the Saviour, the Lord Jesus Christ.   (Philippians 3:20)

Just as our treasures are in heaven:

> But lay up for yourselves treasures in heaven, where neither moth nor rust doth corrupt, and where thieves do not break through nor steal.   (Matthew 6:20)

Just as our home is in heaven:

> Let not your heart be troubled: ye believe in God, believe also in Me. In my Father's house are many mansions: if it were not so, I would have told you. I go to prepare a place for you. And if I go and prepare a place for you, I will come again, and receive you unto myself: that where I am, there ye may be also.
>
> (John 14:1-2)

Just as our hope is in heaven:

> For the hope which is laid up for you in heaven, whereof ye heard before in the word of the truth of the gospel.
>
> (Colossians 1:5)

The wisdom that comes from above is given to us in a book that belongs to another realm. It is the realm of our citizenship, our treasure, our home and our hope. It is the book which contains the truth of that future reality, and through its words, we are enabled to live as pilgrims and strangers here on this earth.

This wisdom then is manifested through God's Son. It is made available through God's Holy Spirit, and it is written down in God's Holy Book, the Bible.

The wise man is the man who has given himself to Jesus Christ and who by the help of the Holy Spirit keeps his intellect in submission to the will of God. Such a man will have the wisdom of God which is from above.

THE SEQUENCE OF HEAVENLY WISDOM

There are seven characteristics of God's wisdom.

1. The Wisdom From Above Is Pure.

This is first in James' list because God's wisdom, like His nature, is based upon the attribute of holiness.

This word for purity and holiness is found in the command of James 4:8 where we are instructed to purify our hearts and turn from duplicity.

There are no hidden motives in God's wisdom. It is transparent and clean. There is nothing under the surface. It is all up front.

The Psalmist reminds us that God's wisdom is just like God's Word for "the commandment of the Lord is pure" (Psalm 19:8).

Purity has no degrees. There is no "positive, comparative, and superlative." There is only the absolute. R. W. Dale reminds us that "Christians are prone to try to escape the dark and ugly stains on their character, but they forget that the nations of the saved in the city of God walk in white raiment and that even the dust of the common earth shows on their clothes and destroys its shining purity."[3]

The wisdom of God which is shown out of our good behavior is *first* pure!

2. The Wisdom From Above Is Peaceable

True peace is always an outgrowth of purity. Peace is a blessing conferred upon us by God, and it is available to us from Him alone. Purity always brings peace. The absence of purity is always accompanied by the absence of peace. Listen to Isaiah:

The Pyramid Of God's Wisdom

Without Hypocrisy

Without Partiality

Full of Mercy and Good Works

Easy to be Entreated

Gentle

Peaceable

Pure

> But the wicked are like the troubled sea, when it cannot rest, whose waters cast up mire and dirt. *There is no peace, saith my God, to the wicked.* (Isaiah 57:20-21)

When the peace of God follows the purity of God's wisdom into our hearts and lives, it will even have an effect on those around us. We will be able to "follow peace with all men" (Hebrews 12:14). We will be able to live peaceably with all men (Romans 12:18). For Christ, who is our Peace, who came into this world as the "Prince of Peace," will be on the throne of our hearts. The "sweet reasonableness" of this peace will cause us to be approachable, to allow discussion, to be willing to yield to others. Such peaceableness will not allow us to drag in personalities nor allow us to make excuses when we are dealing with problems.

John White believes that someone exhibiting this kind of peace will stand out in his world:

> Peace is a kind of lighthouse in the midst of a storm. Winds shriek, waves crash, and lightning flickers all around it, but inside, the children are playing, while their parents go about their work. They may look out the window to marvel at the powers that rage around them, but they have peace. It is the peace of

knowing that the strength that surrounds them is stronger than the strength of the storm.[4]

Isaiah the prophet had this in mind when he wrote:

Thou wilt keep him in perfect peace, whose mind is stayed on thee. (Isaiah 26:3).

And Paul communicates the same idea when he describes this tranquility to the Philippians, "the peace that passeth understanding" (Philippians 4:7). The Psalmist takes us back to the source of peace when he says:

Great peace have they which love thy law, and nothing shall offend them. (Psalm 119:164)

3. The Wisdom From Above Is Gentle

The wisdom of God is first pure and then peaceable and then gentle. According to Matthew Arnold, "Gentleness is sweet reasonableness."[5] It is characteristic of servants. Paul's instruction to Titus bears this out:

To speak evil of no man, to be no brawler, but *gentle*, showing all meekness unto all men. (Titus 3:2)

He said the same thing to Timothy:

And the servant of the Lord must not strive, but be *gentle* unto all men. (2 Timothy 2:24)

Strife is the world's wisdom, but gentleness is a property of the wisdom from above. In the New Testament, the word "gentle" is a word which means, "to know how and when to relax the law, under the pressure of a higher and greater force than the law."

Aristotle put it this way:

Gentleness is equity to pardon human failings, to look to the law giver and not to the law, to the spirit and not to the letter, to the intention and not to the action, to the whole and not to the part, to the character of the person in the long run,and not to the present moment, to remember the good and not the evil.[6]

Carl Sandburg once described Abraham Lincoln as a man of "velvet steel." So a man who operates in the wisdom of God may be a strong, aggressive man, but he will exhibit a sweet gentleness as he deals with people.

I have known two men personally who have vividly embodied this quality in their lives and ministries. The first man is the esteemed pastor or the First Baptist Church of Dallas, Texas, Dr. W. A. Criswell. When as a seminary student I first went to hear him preach, I was almost frightened. He thunders out God's truth. Now in the latter years of his ministry at First Baptist, his presence makes one think of the Holy Righteous God. And yet, sometimes he is so tender and gentle in the pulpit that you sense you are being counseled by a father or grandfather. In Joyce Landorf's language, he is "tough and tender."

Dr. Jerry Falwell is the other man who comes to mind when I review this characteristic of heavenly wisdom. When you see Jerry leading the charge to "clean up America," you have the distinct impression that you wouldn't want to be on the other end of his wrath. But if he comes to your church, as he did to ours recently, he will hug all the children and all the grandmothers and you will marvel at his gentle spirit.

Only the wisdom from God provides such a delicate balance in one's personality. The wisdom of God magnifies our strengths and compensates for our weakness and creates the person God wants us to be.

I believe James alludes to this very quality earlier in his letter:

> Wherefore, my beloved brethren, let every man be swift to hear,
> slow to speak, slow to wrath: for the wrath of man worketh
> not the righteousness of God.　　　　　(James 1:19-20)

4. The Wisdom From Above Is "Easy to be Entreated."

God's wisdom has a conciliatory spirit and is willing to listen to reason. The Greek term that is translated by the phrase, "easy to be entreated," is found only in this verse in the New Testament. It is a military term which means to be willing to take instructions from the Commander-in-Chief. When the spiritually wise man is in command, he must be "gentle." When he is under authority, he must be "easy to be entreated" . . . willing to take instruction.

It is very difficult for many of God's people to be conciliatory. One man I heard about was on his way to church when he stopped by a friend of his who asked, "Where are you going?

"I'm going to a church business meeting," he said.

"What are they voting on?" inquired his friend.

"I don't know," he answered. "Well, then why are you going?" the friend asked.

"To vote against it," he replied.

You wouldn't be laughing now if you were a pastor.

5. The Wisdom From Above Is "Full of Mercy and Good Works."

This characteristic of God's wisdom reminds us that our wisdom is demonstrated by our behavior (James 3:13). Our godly wisdom must be like our love . . . demonstrated in word and in truth. Our lives must back up our testimonies.

When James mentions good works, he touches upon an emphasis that needs revitalization among God's people today. In our determination to keep "good works" out of the gospel message, we have almost removed the term from our vocabularies. But "good works" is an important doctrine for the Christian to understand and practice.

When Paul wrote to the Ephesians, he told them that their salvation was "not of works lest any man should boast" (Ephesians 2:9). But in that same context, he told the Ephesians that they "were created in Christ Jesus *unto* good works" (Ephesians 2:10).

There is a consistent emphasis on this truth in the New Testament:

> And God is able to make all grace abound toward you; that ye, always having all sufficiency in all things, may *abound to every good work*. (2 Corinthians 9:8)

> That ye might walk worthy of the Lord unto all pleasing, *being fruitful in every good work*, and increasing in the knowledge of God. (Colossians 1:10)

> Now our Lord Jesus Christ himself, and God, even our Father . . . comfort your hearts, and stablish you in *every good word and work*. (2 Thessalonians 2:16-17).

> In all things showing thyself a pattern *of good works* . . . (Titus 2:7). Who gave himself for us, that He might redeem us from all iniquity, and purify unto Himself a peculiar people, zealous *of good works*. (Titus 2:14)

> Put them in mind to be subject to principalities and powers and to obey magistrates, *to be ready to every good work*. (Titus 3:1)

> This is a faithful saying, and these things I will that thou affirm constantly, that they who have believed in God might be careful

to maintain good works. These things are good and profitable
unto men.   (Titus 3:8)

Let not a widow be taken into the number under threescore years
old . . . well reported of *for good works.*(1 Timothy 5:9-10)

Charge them that are rich in this world . . . that they *do good*,
that they be rich in *good works.*   (1 Timothy 6:17-18)

In like manner also, that women adorn themselves in modest
apparel . . . which becometh women professing godliness, *with
good works.*   (1 Timothy 2:9-10)

All Scripture is given by inspiration of God . . . That the man
of God may be perfect, thoroughly furnished unto *all good
works.*   (2 Timpthy 3:16-17)

And.let us consider one another to provoke unto love and to
good works.   (Hebrews 10:24)

The consistent message of the Epistle of James is this, "Faith
without works is *dead*" (James 2:20).

6. The Wisdom From Above Is "Without Partiality"

To be impartial is to be straightforward, wholehearted and without
guile. To have respect of persons is the opposite of impartiality and
James says such conduct is sin (James 2:9).

R. W. Dale says that when one has worldly wisdom, it makes him
as shifty as a politician. He sets his sails to the prevailing wind. He
speaks well of a man one day whom he spoke ill of yesterday. Not
because the man changed, but yesterday there was no gain by speaking well of him, and today there is.[7]

Impartiality is just one part of God's wisdom that has been defined
by one as "ethical conduct in harmony with the Word of God."

7. The Wisdom From Above Is "Without Hypocrisy"

Hypocrisy is a word which comes from the world of drama. In
New Testament days, when a person played a part on stage with a
mask, they called him a hypocrite. The term gradually became
associated with folks who played a role off stage as well. Today,
a hypocrite is someone who is not real . . . someone who is phony
and does not truly represent himself.

When Paul wrote to the Romans, he admonished them to love
without hypocrisy (Romans 12:9). Paul would not have qualified
his statements of love with the often used phrase "in the Lord."

TWO KINDS OF WISDOM

	THE WISDOM OF GOD (James 3:17-18)	THE WISDOM OF MAN (James 3:13-16)
SOURCE	"from Above"	"earthly"
QUALITY	"pure"	"sensual"
EXPRESSION	"peaceable"	"bitter envying"
SPIRIT	"gentle"	"devilish"
RECEPTIVITY	"easy to be entreated"	"arrogant boasting"
ACTIVITY	"full of good works"	"every evil work"
RESULT	"peace"	"confusion"

Somehow when I am told that I am loved "in the Lord," I feel like that is a second class kind of love. Many Christians use the phrase to qualify their love, and by doing so they become hypocrites. Godly wisdom never masquerades spirituality when it is operating in the arena of the world, the flesh, and the devil.

THE SEQUEL TO HEAVENLY WISDOM

"And the fruit of righteousness is sown in peace of them that make peace" (James 3:18).

The comparison of heavenly and earthly wisdom is instructive at this juncture. The world's wisdom results in "confusion" (v. 16), but God's wisdom brings "peace" (v. 18). The result of the world's wisdom is "every evil work" (v. 16). We pointed out in the last chapter that this phrase means "every good-for-nothing work." But God's wisdom brings forth fruit. In the fruit of God's wisdom are the seeds of more fruit. "The fruit of righteousness is sown in righteousness" (v. 18). God's wisdom automatically multiplies.

As we look back over this chapter, it becomes evident that wisdom is not so much a "head" matter as it is a "life" matter. It is shown out of our good behavior. James further focuses his attention on one part of our conduct which is more important than the rest. The entire context of this passage on "wisdom" deals with the "tongue," and James would teach us that the part of our behavior that is most critical is our speech. All four of the characteristics of worldly wisdom operate through the tongue. All seven of the characteristics of God's wisdom operate via the tongue. The tongue is the instrument that reveals the source of our wisdom. So, by very careful what you say. You are advertising for your Sponsor!

NOTES

1. Alan Walker, "Beyond Science - What?" *Pulpit Digest* (Sept. 1967), p. 24.

2. Guy King, *A Belief That Behaves* (Fort Washington: Christian Literature Crusade, 1963), p. 73.

3. R.W. Dale, *The Epistle of James* (London: Hodder and Stoughton, 1895), p. 110.

4. John White, "God's Perfect Peace," *Moody Monthly* (Dec. 1962), p. 24.

5. R. W. Dale, *The Epistle of James*, p. 113.

6. Ibid.

7. Ibid., p. 118.

Wisdom For Your Home

"The younger generation no longer respects its elders; it tyrannizes its teachers, fails to rise when older people enter the room and has atrocious manners." No, that comment did not come from a "Letters to the Editor" column in your local newspaper. It is the observation of a wise old gentleman who lived many decades ago . . . Socrates was his name.

These words don't seem too unlike those of a contemporary school teacher who resigned her position in a public school and included this analysis with her resignation:

> The teachers are afraid of the principals, the principals are afraid of the school board, the school board is afraid of the parents, and the parents are afraid of the children. The trouble is, the children are afraid of no one.

From Socrates' day to ours . . . a long jump in history, but just a step where the problems of children are concerned. How to control and discipline children has always ranked near the top of the list of domestic concerns. There are hundreds of theories that in reality can be condensed into *two* basic approaches to the problem. One is the outgrowth of the wisdom of the world which we explored in chapter 3. The other is the product of the wisdom of God which was explained in chapter 4.

The wisdom of the world is the product of Adam and Eve's rebellion against God. From that day in the Garden of Eden until now, humanistic wisdom has ravaged the home. The immediate effect of that first couple's sin is traceable in the Book of Genesis:

Genesis 4 - Lamech becomes a polygamist.
Genesis 9 - Ham looks on his father's nakedness.
Genesis 16 - Abraham has an adulterous affair with Hagar.

Genesis 19 - Homosexuality ravages Sodom.
Genesis 19 - Lot commits incest with his two daughters.
Genesis 20 - Abraham tempts Abimelech to lust after Sarah.
Genesis 25 - Isaac shows preferential treatment for Esau.
Genesis 26 - Isaac follows his father's bad example.
Genesis 34 - Shechem rapes Dinah.
Genesis 37 - Jacob follows Isaac's bad example by showing preferential treatment for Joseph.
Genesis 38 - Judah commits adultery with Tamar.
Genesis 39 - Joseph is falsely accused of attempted rape.

. . . And we are not even out of the book of Genesis . . .

The wisdom of the world turned loose on the home brings about disintegration and destruction. The demise of the American home is the predictable result of having followed the world's wisdom. James describes this wisdom as "bitter envying and strife in your hearts" (James 3:14). He goes on to say that "where envying and strife are, there is confusion and every evil work" (James 3:16).

My book *Before It's Too Late* lists ten signs of deterioration in today's homes. All of these characteristics are the fruit of the world's wisdom:

1. The Disappearance of the Rural Lifestyle
2. The Deregulation of Divorce
3. The Dynamic Singles Explosion
4. The Disregard for the Marriage Ceremony
5. The Development of the ERA
6. The Desensitizing Effect of TV
7. The Defection of the American Father
8. The Determined Interference of the Government
9. The Deterioration of the Public Schools
10. The Discrimination Against the Unborn[1]

Although these characteristics mark our culture, they are not to mark the Christian. We are to live "in the midst of a crooked and perverse nation . . . as lights . . ." (Philippians 2:15). If we follow the truth of God's wisdom, we will certainly be viewed by our contemporaries as "out of touch" with today's scene. We will be branded as irrelevant people who are inordinately tied to the obscure past.

From our sourcebook, the Bible, we receive timeless instructions which, if followed, will set our homes apart in today's world as unique.

The Book of Proverbs is an example. This Old Testament volume contains verse after verse of helpful guidelines for modern Christian parents. Though written by Solomon in a vastly different culture, these wise sayings are as up-to-date as today's family and, believe me, they still work.

Solomon addresses such issues as family problems, sexual deviation, adulterous women, education in the home, rebellious children, parent-child relationships, and many, many others. The age old writer reminds us that:

> Through wisdom is a house builded and by understanding it
> is established: and by knowledge shall the chambers be filled
> with precious and pleasant riches.   (Proverbs 24:3-4)

Literally the proverb says, "Through wisdom is a house *rebuilt.*" From the wisdom of God it is possible to glean principles that will put our homes back together.

In this chapter we will explore just one narrow corridor of God's wisdom . Besides being helpful to all of us, this brief inductive study will also serve as an illustration of God's wisdom at work in many areas of home life. If you haven't already done so, I would urge you to begin making an indepth study of the principles for family living found in the Book of Proverbs.

DISCIPLINE OF CHILDREN

From the day our first child was born, I have been very interested in the subject of discipline. With four children still at home, you can be sure that I continue to be a student of the subject. I have read everything from Spock to Dobson and I must confess that there are still many facets of this subject that baffle me.

I was both surprised and delighted when I discovered how much information God had put in His Word to help us become good disciplinarians.

First of all, Solomon puts discipline back into perspective by reinforcing the idea of positive discipline:

> Train up a child in the way he should go and when he is old,
> he will not depart from it.   (Proverbs 22:6)

Discipline first of all involves the structuring of our children's lives so that they move along a positive, predetermined course. God has

TWO KINDS OF DISCIPLINE

set the perimeters of that course and he expects Christian parents to make sure that way is followed.

This is what Paul had in mind as he wrote to the Ephesian fathers:

> And, ye fathers, provoke not your children to wrath, but bring them up in the nurture and admonition of the Lord.
>
> (Ephesians 6:4)

The idea here seems to be that it is possible to overdo the negative part of discipline while ignoring the important positive dimension. If we are not careful, we will spend all of our time "putting our children down" and not enough time "bringing them up."

Perhaps you will identify with this illustration. You are seated at the dinner table in your home. Your four small children, ranging in age from two years to ten, are just beginning to devour the evening meal. As you casually observe the whole scene, you notice that your four-year-old has just put his glass of milk down very near to the edge of the table. He has also strategically located it in the flight pattern of his right arm. You know what is about to take place. You have seen it all before, many times. What do you do?

You have several options. First of all, you might speak sharply, warning him in no uncertain terms of the consequences that await if the inevitable takes place. You then wait until, sure enough, he knocks his milk off on the floor. True to your word, you dish out every single nuance of judgment that was promised. After all, he must learn that "crime does not pay."

But let me suggest another alternative. Why not reach out and move his milk to a safe position on the table? When you see him move toward disaster, reach out and take hold of his arm in order to prevent the accident.

Why is it that we have developed such capacity for the punitive action and so little for the positive direction that also falls under the heading of "discipline" in God's Word?

When I was a college student, I traveled during one summer vacation with the official college quartet. One of the members of that quartet was a red-headed pianist named Rich. To say that he kept us loose is to put it mildly. He saw humor in things that passed the rest of us right by.

When we were singing in Fort Wayne, Indiana on one occasion, Rich pulled a stunt that reminds me now of the way so many families operate in the area of discipline. After working out at the downtown YMCA, we were standing on the corner waiting for the light to change. Rich saw something that all of the rest of us missed. Reconstructing it, after the fact, we all realized what had happened.

Just before the light turned red to stop a lady driving a late model car had pulled too far forward and was blocking the crosswalk. When she realized what had happened, she put her car in reverse and backed up. What she did next only Rich had seen. Just before the light turned green, he poked me in the ribs and said, "Watch this," pointing to the woman's car.

Sure enough, just as the signal changed, she stepped on the gas and instead of going forward, she plowed into the car behind her. She had forgotten to put her car back in forward drive. No one was hurt, but we sure saw a lot of chrome and glass redistributed.

Now why would anybody do something like that? Wouldn't it make sense to warn her before she made that mistake? To this day I don't know why he didn't shout at her. But the point is, why do we as parents often say to each other, "watch this" instead of providing the necessary strong guidance to keep our children out of trouble. Mark it down . . . discipline is positive and positive discipline works.

The American Institute of Family Relations reported a survey in which mothers were asked to keep track of the number of times they made negative and positive comments to their children. They discovered that they criticized ten times for every one time that they said something favorable.

Teachers apparently do a little better. A three-year survey of the Orlando Florida Public Schools found that the teachers were only seventy-five percent negative. The study indicated that it takes four positive statements from the teacher to offset the effects of one negative statement to a child.

I have taken so much space to emphasize the importance of positive discipline so that what follows will not be taken as a distorted view of the subject. These eight principles which we now explore are totally opposed to the current humanistic philosophy. Basically they answer the question, "Should parents ever spank their children?" The Bible says "yes," and in Proverbs, Ephesians, and Hebrews, it gives the principles that follow.

1. Discipline Is Proper For Every Child
"If ye endure chastening, God dealeth with you as with sons; for what son is he whom the Father chasteneth not" (Heb. 12:7).

No matter how big, how strong, or how mean, *every* child is to be under discipline. What is happening in this world of ours that is dominated by humanistic philosophy is the accumulated effect of several generations of young people who have not been under any discipline. In the name of freedom we have turned them loose too soon, and we are living with the sad result of our negligence.

Paul Harvey expressed the convictions of many of us when he said,

> I'm against giving youth more freedom. They're already about as free as an unguided missile. Jesus didn't campaign for unlimited freedom. He bound himself to God's will. We need some Christian youth with direction and purpose and faith and dedication, and that's born in the home.

2. Discipline Proves Our Love For Our Children
He that spareth the rod hateth his son; but he that loveth him chasteneth him early (Proverbs 13:24).

Do you remember your parents saying something like this, "I'm going to discipline you and I want you to know that it's because I love you." Or maybe this sticks in your mind as it does mine, "This

PRINCIPLES FOR DISCIPLINE

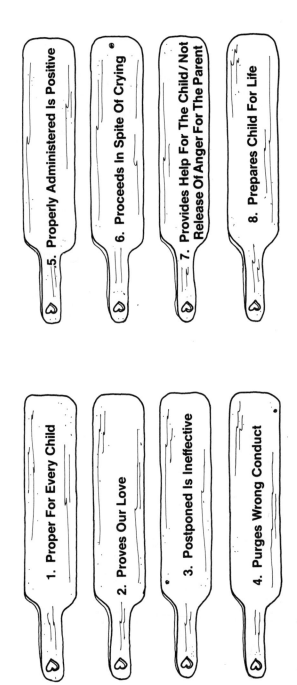

1. Proper For Every Child

2. Proves Our Love

3. Postponed Is Ineffective

4. Purges Wrong Conduct

5. Properly Administered Is Positive

6. Proceeds In Spite Of Crying

7. Provides Help For The Child / Not Release Of Anger For The Parent

8. Prepares Child For Life

hurts me more than it does you." That last statement seemed to always be reserved for the introductory remarks before an especially eloquent spanking.

Now that I'm a parent I realize how right my parents were. Some of the most painful moments in my life as a father have been during the administration of discipline at home. But listen, God says that the exercise of godly discipline is the proof of our love for our children.

Isn't it interesting that the number one reason parents give for not spanking their children is "because they love them too much?" Yet God says that refusing to discipline evidences not our love, but our hate.

Dr. James Dobson in his best seller, *Dare to Discipline,* has written that:

> The parent has got to convince himself that discipline is not something that he does to the child, but something he does for the child. His attitude toward the child must be, "I love you too much to let you behave like that."[2]

Dobson goes on to explain how parents of little children can communicate the whole concept of loving discipline by telling them this little story:

> I knew of a little birdie once who was in his nest with his mommy. The mommy bird went off to find some worms to eat. She told the little bird not to get out of the nest while she was gone, but the little bird didn't mind her and he jumped out of the nest and fell to the ground and a big cat got him.[3]

Dobson suggests translating the story into the life of the little child by saying:

> When I tell you to mind me it's because I know what's best for you just as the mother bird did with the little birdie. When I tell you to stay in the front yard, it's because I want you to be careful not to run into the street and get hit by a car. I love you. I don't want anything to happen to you and if you don't mind me, I'll have to spank you to help you remember how important it is. Do you understand?[4]

You might not tell your children such a parable at the moment of discipline, but I hope you communicate your love for them especially at that time. I have found that a strong expression of love immediately after administering a spanking has been a very special moment with my children.

One of our children is very strong-willed and her strength is never more evident than when she is being spanked. She absolutely refuses to cry. No matter how hard she is spanked, she *will not* shed a tear or show any emotion. But as soon as the spanking is over and I put my arms around her and tell her that I love her, she comes unglued. In the end, it's the love that comes through to our children. God Himself teaches us this as He deals with those of us who are His sons:

> For whom the Lord loveth, He chasteneth and scourgeth every son whom He receiveth. (Hebrews 12:6)

3. Discipline Postponed Will Be Ineffective

Chasten thy son while there is hope, and let not thy soul spare for his crying (Proverbs 19:18).

On one occasion a mother came to me and asked when she should begin to discipline her children. "How old are they?" I asked. "They are nine and eleven," she replied. I had to tell her that she was already too late.

Some psychologists have suggested that the troubled teenage years are just a condensation of all the discipline that has or has not been administered in the earlier years of the child's life. When you examine what some parents are told by modern psychologists, you can understand why discipline is postponed and avoided. There are so many conflicting ideas in the great mass of man's wisdom that the only option left to the modern secular parent is to put all the various theories in a hat and pull one out at random. These diverse ideas have only one common denominator . . . their origin. They are the product of *this* world and man's wisdom.

In a recent issue of the secular magazine, *Psychology Today*, the Prentice-Hall book by John V. Flowers and Bernard Schwartz was reviewed. The book is entitled, *Are You a Newrotic?* It is a wild and zany collection of new emotional disturbances which have supposedly surfaced in southern California, thus the name "newrotic."

One of the "newrosis" for the eighties is a malady called "permissive parent burnout." According to Flowers and Schwartz, it occurs in those who think their parents were tyrants and who therefore wish to rear their children more liberally.

For our benefit they included the following case study:

> I swore I would never treat my children the way my parents treated me. So I prepared myself. I read all of the latest child-rearing books: *Discipline Can Be Fun*; *The Children's Liberation Movement Handbook*; and *Toilet Training Your Teenager*. I did everything the books told me. If my kids misbehaved, I never spanked them or stood them in the corner—I shared my feelings with them: "It worries me when you set the drapes on fire." "I'm concerned that you've been gone for a week without calling home."
>
> I never told them "because I said so" when they asked why they had to do something. Instead, I explained things to them. When my son was poking his little sister in the eye, I said, "Eyes are very sensitive, and when you do that it hurts." He poked her in the other eye.
>
> Finally things got so bad, I went to a psychologist. He told me to ignore the children when they misbehaved and to praise them if they behaved appropriately. Now the county social worker has accused me of neglect.
>
> Recently, some authority on nutrition was interviewed on a talk show, and he said that kids act crazy when you feed them too much sugar-coated cereal. So I switched to honey. They poured a jar of it on the dog. Right now I'm building a woodshed.[5]

Those of us who know the Bible could have saved our poor fictitious friend a lot of trouble. She ended up where we start.

4. Discipline Purges Wrong Conduct From A Child's Life

*Foolishness is bound in the heart of a child, but the rod of correction shall drive it far from him (*Proverbs 22:15).

I love the story about the mother of three very small children who was trying to get ready to go out with her husband for a late dinner engagement. The children, who all slept in the same room, were playing the games all children play. They would not quiet down. They continued to talk and laugh and get in and out of bed even though they were threatened regularly by their irritated mother. Finally, when she had had all she could stand, she went to the bottom of the stairs and shouted, "If I hear one more word out of any of you, I'm coming upstairs."

Everything quieted down for about five short minutes and then gradually the noise level began to build again. True to her promise, mom grabbed a towel and wrapped it around her head which had been totally immersed in the kitchen sink in the rinsing stage of her shampoo. Up the stairs she stomped and into the room which by now had gotten very quiet.

"I'm not coming up here again. Now you kids stay in bed and be quiet." The silence was deafening as she walked out of the room, but as she stood outside the door for a moment, she heard the littlest of the children ask, "Who was that?"

Now I suppose something could be said for scaring our children into obedience and submission, but I doubt if we could create enough disguises to last very long. God has a better way. The application of the board of education to the seat of knowledge works wonders.

The Psalmist states something similar to Solomon when he writes, "It is good for me that I have been afflicted, that I might learn thy statutes" (Psalms 119:71). He confesses earlier in this same Psalm that "Before I was afflicted, I went astray, but now I have kept thy word" (Psalms 119:67).

Now add to these two verses, this one:

> Now no chastening for the present seemeth to be joyous, but grievous; nevertheless, afterward it yieldeth the peaceable fruit of righteousness unto which that are exercised thereby.
>
> (Hebrews 12:11)

An unknown humorist has summarized the problem by pointing out that a great deal of today's juvenile delinquency is the result of parents trying to train their children without starting at the *bottom*.

5. Discipline Properly Administered Will Not Hurt Your Child
Withhold not correction from the child; for if thou beatest him with the rod, he shall not die (Proverbs 23:13).

On numerous occasions, I have been told by honest parents that the reason they don't discipline their children is because they fear they may cause some physical harm. Let's face it, we've been all over the ball park on this issue. We've come through the permissive age of no corporal discipline and into the present age of the child abuse syndrome. We didn't spank our children then because we didn't believe in it. We don't spank them now for fear that someone will report us to the authorities.

If we are really honest, most of us do such an inadequate job of discipline not out of the fear of hurting our children but rather out of the refusal to inconvenience ourselves. We yell at our children from the other end of the house because we are too lazy to walk to their rooms and deal with the problem. We let internal tensions get out of hand because in order to deal with the problem we would have to leave our favorite seat in front of the televised pro football game. Discipline requires a certain amount of inconvenience and many of us are just too lazy to get at it.

6. Discipline Proceeds In Spite Of Crying

Chasten thy son while there is hope, and let not thy soul spare for his crying (Proverbs 19:18).

Our smallest child seems to be way ahead of this proverb. He cries before the discipline is administered. With him, we get the result before the action. But I've already alluded to another member of our family who doesn't even cry when the discipline has been hard. Crying is really a very poor indicator of the pain that is inflicted. Children who treat their bodies brutally in outdoor sports without so much as a minor complaint can begin to shed tears at the drop of a hat if the connotation of discipline is attached to the pain. This proverb simply reminds us that tears cannot be the barometer of successful discipline.

7. Discipline Provides Help For The Child, Not Release Of Anger For The Adult

And, ye fathers, provoke not your children to wrath, but bring them up in the nurture and admonition of the Lord (Ephesians 6:4).

Dr. Haddon Robinson, the President of Conservative Baptist Seminary, in some unpublished notes on Ephesians 6:4, writes this:

> Even though I am to punish my youngsters, I must be certain that the discipline is for their positive good. All of us can sympathize with the mother who said in exasperation, 'Well the kids were making such a racket that I went in and spanked them . . . it didn't help much but it sure did me a world of good.' Too often we spank our children because we are irritated, or we scold them and nag at them to release our own frustrations. Chastening and admonitions require thought and spiritual sensitivity if it is to be of the Lord. My discipline, no matter what

it is, should be designed to bring my children to God. In all of the passages about discipline in the Scripture, not one that I know of says that discipline is exclusively to penalize. It is always used in the positive context of instruction, and correction. It should never be an occasion for a parent to take out his anger or his own irritation on the child.[6]

8. Discipline Prepares A Child For The Most Important Decision In His Life

Thou shalt beat him with the rod, and shalt deliver his soul from hell (Proverbs 23:14).

Positive corrective discipline within the home provides the kind of atmosphere that makes it most possible for a child to come to a personal decision about God. Although there are many who come to Christ in the middle or later years of life, the vast majority of Christians in our churches are Christians as the result of growing up in a structured Christian home where some form of discipline was practiced. Parents who teach their children love by caring enough to confront them in their sin, also teach them much about their Heavenly Father who is just like that.

These eight principles reveal the wisdom of God at work in the home. As you no doubt have observed, they are in total contrast to what the world's psychologists are telling us. Who is right? It seems to me that our generation has graphically demonstrated the result of trying to rear children by the wisdom of the world.

There are still only two ways to operate within your home . . . God's way and man's. The result of your choice is powerfully illustrated in the brief history of these two families.

> Max Jukes lived in the state of New York. He did not believe in Christian training. He married a girl of similar background and from this union, 1026 descendants have been studied. Three-hundred of them died prematurely, one-hundred were sent to the penitentiary, 90 were public prostitutes. There were one hundred drunkards and the family cost the state one million two hundred thousand dollars. They made little contribution to society. They believed in the wisdom of the world.
>
> In that same state lived Jonathan Edwards, the great Puritan preacher. He believed in Christian training and he married a girl of similar beliefs and character. From this union, seven-hundred and twenty-five descendants have been studied. Out of this family have come three-hundred preachers, sixty-five

college professors, thirteen university presidents, sixty authors of good books, three United States Congressmen, and one Vice-President of the United States. And outside of Aaron Burr, a grandson of Jonathan Edwards, the family has not caused the state one bit of trouble, or cost the state a single dollar.[7]

The great difference in the two families is certainly not a coincidence. The difference is the result of a decision made early in the life of each family. And you, too, must choose whether to follow man's wisdom or God's in your home.

NOTES

1. David Jeremiah, *Before It's Too Late* (Nashville: Thomas Nelson Pub., 1982), pp. 17-32.

2. James C. Dobson, *Dare To Discipline* (Wheaton: Tyndale House, 1971), pp. 29-30.

3. Ibid.

4. Ibid.

5. John V. Flowers and Bernard Schwarts, *"Are You A Newrotic?" Psychology For Today* (March 1984), p. 17.

6. Haddon Robinson, Unpublished notes, Dallas Theological Seminary.

7. Paul Lee Tan, *Encyclopedia of 7,700 Illustrations* (Rochville, Maryland: Assurance Pub., 1979), pp. 961-962.

6

Wisdom—One Man Who Prayed For It And Got It

What do you dream of? What keeps you awake at night? What motivation is so strong within you that it blots out all others? Some anonymous thinker has written:

Tell me your dreams, and I will read the riddle of your life. Tell me your prayers, and I will write the history of your soul. Tell me your askings, and I will tell you your gettings. Tell me what you seek, and I will tell you what you are . . . I do not wish to know your possessions . . . only your wants. I do not care to know what you have, only what you have not and desire to have; not your attainments, but what you have not yet attined and follow after. That which comes to you in your victories by day and your dreams by night, the ideal you set before you, the things you approve as excellent, what you seek after and have given your heart to, these are the measure of a man.

In a truer sense than Shakespeare meant, "We are such stuff as dreams are made of." Dreams may have no price in the market, but they alone give dignity to life.

If these words are a true assessment of the value of dreams, what can we say about the dream of Solomon recorded in 1 Kings chapter 3:

And Solomon loved the Lord, walking in the statutes of David his father: only he sacrificed and burnt incense in high places. And the king went to Gibeon to sacrifice there; for that was the great high place: a thousand burnt offerings did Solomon offer upon that altar. In Gibeon the Lord appeared to Solomon in a dream by night: and God said, Ask what I shall give thee.

And Solomon said, Thou has showed unto thy servant David my father great mercy, according as he walked before thee in truth, and in righteousness, and uprightness of heart with thee; and thou hast kept for him this great kindness, that thou hast given him a son to sit on his throne, as it is this day. And now O Lord my God, thou hast made thy servant king instead of David my father: and I am but a little child: I know not how to go out or come in. And thy servant is in the midst of thy people which thou hast chosen, a great people, that cannot be numbered nor counted for multitude. Give therefore thy servant an understanding heart to judge thy people, that I may discern between good and bad: for who is able to judge this thy so great a people? And the speech pleased the Lord, that Solomon had asked this thing. And God said unto him, Because thou hast asked this thing, and hast not asked for thyself long life; neither hast asked riches for thyself, nor hast asked the life of thine enemies; but hast asked for thyself understanding to discern judgment; Behold I have done according to thy words: lo, I have given thee a wise and an understanding heart; so that there was none like thee before thee, neither after thee shall any arise like unto thee. And I have also given thee that which thou hast not asked, both riches, and honor: so that there shall not be any among the kings like unto thee all thy days. And if thou wilt walk in my ways, to keep my statutes and my commandments, as thy father David did walk, then I will lengthen thy days. And Solomon awoke; and behold it was a dream. And he came to Jerusalem, and stood before the ark of the covenant of the Lord, and offered up burnt offerings, and offered peace offerings, and made a feast to all his servants.

(I Kings 3:3-15)

I am not irreverent when I say that the Lord Jesus never dreamed a dream better than Solomon's dream. Lord Melbourne of England was so gripped by Solomon's dream that after Princess Victoria was proclaimed the Queen of England, Melbourne opened his Bible and read to the young queen the entire story of Solomon's dream.

It at once becomes obvious to us that Solomon was reflecting in his prayer the first two keys of wisdom mentioned in chapter 2.

Note, first of all, his *humble spirit*. Solomon's words are expressive. "I am but a little child, I know not how to go out or come in . . . I am in the midst of thy people whom thou hast chosen, a great people, who cannot be numbered or counted for multitude. . . ."

Any man who is on the threshold of a great enterprise and does not possess a humble spirit is certain to fail. One of the best forecasts of the success of Solomon is that he saw the magnitude of the work God had called him to do, and realized his own insufficiency and dependency upon his God.

Secondly, notice Solomon's *hungry soul.* "Give therefore thy servant an understanding heart that I may discern between good and bad. For who is able to judge this thy so great a people?" (I Kings 3:9).

He did not ask for long life, for his hunger was to live right rather than to live long. Methuselah lived nine hundred years and apparently never said a word worth putting down in the Bible.

Solomon did not ask for riches or even for the life of his enemies. He hungered to know God in a dynamic way so that he would be able to be God's man among his people. The Bible says that the request pleased God (1 Kings 3:10), and that God answered his request and that he gave him both riches and honor along with wisdom (v. 13).

One of the amazing things about Solomon's prayer is the fact that he was only twenty-years-old when he prayed this prayer. I don't know about you, but when I remember what I was like at age twenty, I am even more amazed at Solomon's request.

What would cause a young man to reflect such maturity in the midst of so many tremendously tempting options? Perhaps even his name is a clue. "Solomon," which means "peace" or "peaceable," was the tenth son of David and the second son of David and Bethsheba. He was also known as Jedediah . . . "beloved of the Lord" (I Kings 1:11-12).

He was very uniquely prepared of God. Alexander Whyte summarized Solomon's special position in the kingdom:

> If ever any young saint sought first the kingdom of God and His righteousness, and had all these things added to Him, it was Solomon . . . If ever there was anyone of whom it could be said that he had attained, and was already perfect, it was Solomon. If ever a blazing lighthouse was set up in the sea of life to warn every man, it was Solomon . . . If ever it was said over any child's birth, where sin abounded, grace did much more abound, it was surely over Solomon.[1]

SPIRITUAL INFLUENCES
THAT PREPARED SOLOMON

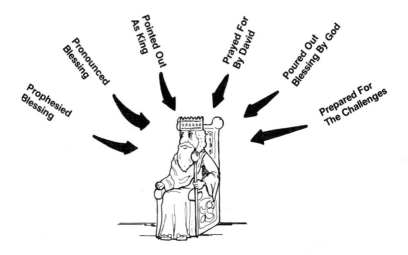

Reading through the history of Solomon's family, it is possible to identify at least six spiritual influences that impacted his life and produced his early maturity.

1. God Prophesied Blessing Upon Him Before He Was Born.

Behold a son shall be born to thee, who shall be a man of rest; and I will give him rest from all his enemies round about; for his name shall be Solomon; and I will give peace and quietness unto Israel in his days, He shall build a house for my name; and shall be my son, and I will be his father, and I will establish the throne of his kingdom over Israel forever.

(1 Chronicles 22:9-10)

2. God Pronounced Blessing Upon Him At His Birth.

. . . and the Lord loved him. And he sent by the hand of Nathan the prophet; and he called his name Jedidiah, because of the Lord. (2 Samuel 12:24-25)

3. God Pointed Him Out As Israel's King.

Furthermore, David the king said unto all the congregation, Solomon my son, *whom alone God hath chosen*, is yet young and tender. (1 Chronicles 29:1)

4. David Prayed For God's Blessing To Be Upon Him.

> And give unto Solomon my son a perfect heart, to keep thy commandments, thy testimonies, and thy statutes, and to do all these things, and to build the palace, for which I have made provision. (1 Chronicles 29:19)

Bible students believe that Psalm 72 is another recorded prayer of David, on behalf of his son.

5. God Poured Out A Special Blessing Upon Solomon When He came King.

> And the Lord magnified Solomon exceedingly in the sight of all Israel, and bestowed upon him such royal majesty as had not been on any king before him in Israel.(1 Chronicles 29:25)

6. David Prepared Him For The Challenges He Would Face As King.

> And thou, Solomon my son, know thou the God of thy father, and serve Him with a perfect heart and with a willing mind: for the Lord searcheth all hearts and understandeth all the imaginations of the thoughts: if thou seek him, he will be found of thee; but if thou forsake him, he will cast thee off forever. Take heed now; for the Lord hath chosen thee to build a house for the sanctuary: be strong and do it.(1 Chronicles 28:9-10)

So when young Solomon prayed, he brought together in his prayer all the influences that had been preparing him for his moment of leadership. In his prayer, he followed his father's instructions to seek the Lord. The result of it all was this response from his Heavenly Father:

> Behold, I have done according to thy words: Lo, I have given thee a wise and an understanding heart; so that there was none like thee before thee, neither after thee shall any arise like unto thee. (1 Kings 3:12)

Solomon then became the wisest man ever to live. The Scriptures document this statement, not in an isolated text, but in several very clear statements:

> So King Solomon exceeded all the kings of the earth for riches and for wisdom. And all the earth sought to Solomon to hear his wisdom, which God had put in his heart.(1 Kings 10:23-24)

> And God gave Solomon wisdom and understanding exceeding

much, and largeness of heart, even as the sand that is on the seashore. And Solomon's wisdom excelled the wisdom of all the children of the east country, and all the wisdom of Egypt. For he was wiser than all men . . . And his fame was in all nations round about . . . And there came of all people to hear the wisdom of Solomon, from all kings of the earth, which had heard of his wisdom.   (1 Kings 4:29-31, 34)

The most powerful testimony to the wisdom of Solomon comes from a foreign witness. When the Queen of Sheba heard about Solomon's wisdom, she couldn't believe her ears, so she decided to see for herself. She made the long journey to Solomon's palace and after thoroughly investigating his reputation, filed this report:

> . . . it was a true report that I heard in mine own land of thy acts and of thy wisdom. Howbeit I believed not the words, until I came, and mine eyes had seen it: and, behold, the half was not told me: thy wisdom and prosperity exceedeth the fame which I heard. Happy are thy men, happy are these thy servants, which stand continually before thee, and that hear thy wisdom. Blessed be the Lord thy God, which delighted in thee, to set thee on the throne of Israel because the Lord loved Israel forever, therefore made he thee king to do judgment and justice.
> (1 Kings 10:6-9)

It is accurate to say that all rivers ran into Solomon's sea; wisdom and knowledge, wine and women, wealth and fame, music and songs. Though it would be impossible to describe the vast boundaries of his wisdom, it is within the scope of this study to indicate some of the more obvious evidences of Solomon's God-given understanding.

HIS INSIGHT INTO PROBLEMS

Immediately following the record of Solomon's prayer for wisdom is the story of his first major decision as a king. A situation developed in which there were no witnesses . . . just the contestants (1 Kings 3:16-28). Two mothers who lived together in the same house had children born to them and on a given night, one of the children died. Both mothers claimed the living child. Nobody knew anything about the situation but the two women, and they came before the king.

The first woman claimed that her baby still lived. She said, "This woman lost her baby. It died while I was asleep, and she came and took my living baby in its place and after awhile when I was awakened, I looked intently at this baby in my arms and found it dead, but it was not my baby.

The other mother denied this version of the incident and claimed the living baby as her own.

Now under the law, everything is confirmed by two or three witnesses. But there is no evidence except the testimony of the two parties in contention. How did the young king handle this impossible problem?

Watch him in action! He said, "Bring a sword to me." The sword was brought. "Cut the baby in half and give each woman one-half of the baby," he commanded.

Would Solomon have carried out that barbarous deed? I think not! He was just collecting evidence.

As soon as he gave his orders, one women said, "No, don't kill the baby. Let her have the child," and pointed to her adversary.

"Yes, kill the baby," said the other woman, "and give each of us half of the child."

Now Solomon had his evidence. He knew what to do. He gave the verdict, "Give the baby to the woman who prefers to lose the child than to see it slain. She is without question the real mother."

The first decision of Solomon had an overwhelming impact upon Israel:

> And all Israel heard of the judgments which the king had judged
> and they feared the king; for they saw that the wisdom of God
> was in him to do judgment. (1 Kings 3:28)

HIS INTEREST IN NATURE.

> And (Solomon) spake of trees, from the cedar tree that is in
> Lebanon even unto the hyssop that springeth out of the wall:
> he spake also of beasts, and of fowl, and of creeping things,
> and of fishes. (1 Kings 4:33)

Solomon was an expert in natural history, zoology, ornithology and botany. In fact, he was the world's first great naturalist. His references to nature are abundant in the Proverbs alone.

Solomon's love for nature was so well established in his day that a number of traditions grew up around him. Though these traditions were not based upon fact, they do illustrate how Solomon's contemporaries understood his love for the world of nature created by God.

One such tradition said that the birds loved Solomon so much that the doves would form a canopy with outspread wings under which he would march from his house to the temple. You need not believe this legend, but it does show what the people thought of Solomon's knowledge and love of nature. He could get at the secret of the plant on the wall and the cedar of Lebanon and the birds that fly and the flowers that bloom.

HIS INTERPRETATION OF RIDDLES

The Queen of Sheba went to see Solomon to "prove him with hard questions" (I Kings 10:1). Actually, the phrase "hard questions" refers to riddles . . . hard questions. Recently at our house, we have been caught up in "biblical riddles." You know the rather humorous riddles like:

Riddle:	When did five Old Testament people sleep in bed?
Answer:	When Abraham slept with his "forefathers."
Riddle:	Why couldn't Noah play cards?
Answer:	Because his wife was sitting on the deck.
Riddle:	When is a motorcycle mentioned in the Bible?
Answer:	When the noise of David's triumph was heard throughout the land.
Riddle:	Who was the smallest man in the Bible?
Answer:	Ne-hi-miah

I'm sure Solomon's questions were much more challenging and worthwhile than these.

The queen communed with Solomon of all that was in her heart (1 Kings 10:2). Solomon responded by telling her "all her questions: there was not any thing hid from the king, which he told her not" (1 Kings 10:3).

Someone has jokingly commented that Solomon, with this accomplishment, set himself apart for all time as the only man who ever lived, who answered completely all the questions put to him by a woman.

HIS INCREDIBLE WEALTH

Solomon's kingdom was worthy of a king whose wisdom eclipsed the wisdom of all other kings on earth. He possessed great volumes of gold, silver, precious stones, and spices. He owned servants, cupbearers, and gorgeous clothes. He enjoyed rich cuisine, officers in costly uniforms, horses, and chariots. At the height of his rule, he fed ten thousand people from his private kitchen daily. He received a foreign tribute of at least ten million per year. His father, David, had bequeathed him an estimated five billion dollars in gold, silver, brass, and iron; and Solomon added to it out of his own treasury so that the temple could be built.

When Solomon's magnificent temple was built, only seven years were needed to complete the task. So extravagant was the preparation for the construction of the temple that Solomon could boast that neither hammer nor axe, nor any iron tool, was heard in the temple while it was being built. Only a builder can adequately imagine the expertise and extravagant expense that this required.

HIS INSPIRED WRITINGS

Solomon was the original fountainhead of Old Testament wisdom. According to I Kings 4:32, he spoke 3,000 proverbs and wrote 1,005 songs. The writings of Solomon which are included in the Bible are:

> Song of Solomon
> Proverbs
> Ecclesiastes
> Psalm 72
> Psalm 127

We know that there was much more that Solomon wrote than that which is contained in the sacred Scriptures. Proverbs has only 915 verses in all, so less than a third of the almost 3,000 proverbs which Solomon spoke are preserved for us.

Here, then, was a man who prayed for wisdom and God granted his petition. The Lord gave this man above and beyond all he could ask or think. As we shall learn in the next chapter, Solomon, in the end, perverted his God-given gift and ended his life in disgrace. But even his fall into sin does not diminish what God did for Solomon when he asked in faith for God's wisdom.

You may be wondering if God is still in the habit of granting answers to such humble prayers for wisdom.

There is a statement from our Lord Himself that emphatically answers your question. In referring to the visit of the Queen of Sheba to Solomon's palace, Jesus said:

> The queen of the south shall rise up in the judgment with this generation, and shall condemn it: for she came from the uttermost parts of the earth to hear the wisdom of Solomon, and behold, a greater than Solomon is here.   (Matthew 12:42)

Who is the "greater-than-Solomon" about whom Jesus spoke? It is Jesus Christ Himself. He is the one whose wisdom makes Solomon's fade in comparison. Isaiah the prophet described Jesus Christ like this:

> And the Spirit of the Lord shall rest upon him, the *spirit of wisdom and understanding,* the spirit of *counsel* and might, the spirit of knowledge and of the fear of the Lord. (Isaiah 11:2)

In 1 Corinthians 1:24 we read, "But unto them who are called, both Jews and Greeks, Christ the power of God, and the wisdom of God." Your "Solomon" is the Lord Jesus Christ to whom you may come with the same "hard questions" as those brought by the Queen of the South to Solomon. Be sure that He will answer everything that your heart may bring to Him.

H. J. Horn eloquently urges us to seek the wisdom found in the Lord:

> If before the wise man who became a fool; if before the Proverb-maker who himself became a Proverb; if before the richly endowed man whose glorious abilities were lent to utter folly of idolatry; if before the king whose kingliness became vanity, the Queen of the South bowed herself; how much more should we bow before the unfading wisdom, the unsullied purity, and the eternal kingship of the Lord of all. Let us enthrone Him on the throne of our hearts who has become to us the wisdom of God.

WHERE CAN WISDOM BE FOUND?

> But though men can do all these things, they don't know where to find wisdom and understanding. They not only don't know how to get it, but, in fact, it is not to be found among the living.
>
> "It's not here," the oceans say; and the seas reply, "Nor is it here."

It cannot be bought for gold or silver, nor for all the gold of Ophir or precious onyx stones or sapphires. Wisdom is far more valuable than gold and glass. It cannot be bought for jewels mounted in fine gold. Coral or crystal is worthless in trying to get it; its price is far above rubies. Topaz from Ethiopia cannot purchase it, nor even the purest gold.

Then where can we get it? Where can it be found? For it is hid from the eyes of all mankind; even the sharp-eyed birds in the sky cannot discover it.

But Destruction and Death speak of knowing something about it! And God surely knows where it is to be found, for he looks throughout the whole earth, under all the heavens. He makes the winds blow and sets the boundaries of the oceans. He makes the laws of the rain and a path for the lightning. He knows where wisdom is and declares it to all who will listen. He established it and examined it thoroughly. And this is what he says to all mankind: "Look, to fear the Lord is true wisdom: to forsake evil is real understanding."

Job 28:12-28 (The Living Bible)

NOTE

1. Alexander Whyte, *Bible Characters—The Old Testament* (Grand Rapids: Zondervan, 1964), p. 278.

7

When Wisdom Was Not Enough

When the history of my generation has been written, one of the saddest chapters will concern the moral defeat of many of our Christian leaders. Hardly a month passes without the news of some respected leader's fall into disobedience and sin.

Some of these men have been personal friends of mine, and I have known them to be men who enjoyed the blessing of God upon their lives and ministries. Now they have been set aside. Some have repented and been restored to a measure of usefulness in the kingdom. Others have stubbornly refused to face their sin, and are living as pagans in the world.

Each time that news reaches me about another fallen warrior, I find myself reflecting on Solomon. No man enjoyed the blessing of God upon his life and ministry as did Israel's wisest king. The greatness that was prophesied of him before his birth was fully realized during the glory days of his administration. He was, according to the testimony of his contemporaries, the wisest and wealthiest king who ever lived. And yet, with all his advantages and successes, in the end he failed God and made a fool of himself.

As we open the Bible to 1 Kings chapter 6, we see the first of two things that caused his downfall.

HE HAD AN INCREDIBLE APPETITE FOR WEALTH

He had been given so much by God, and yet, his whole life seems to be characterized by his lust and greed for more. An illustration of that is graphically presented to us at the end of 1 Kings 6 and the beginning of 1 Kings 7.

1 Kings 6:37-38 records the fact that the construction of God's house, the temple, took seven years to complete. An unfortunate chapter division tends to hide the contrasting statement contained in 1 Kings 7:1:

> But Solomon was building his own house thirteen years, and he finished all his house.

We dare not make more out of this than we should, but, we cannot help observe that Solomon took twice as long to build his own house as he did to build the house of God. He also lavished upon his own house wealth, and beauty, and riches.

As we advance to the tenth chapter of 1 Kings, the evidence mounts:

> Now the weight of gold that came to Solomon in one year was six hundred, three-score and six talents of gold.(1 Kings 10:14)

This was the tribute which Solomon exacted from the heathen nations around him. Verse 18 of this chapter describes Solomon's throne as being ivory, covered with gold.

Verse 21 adds this astounding truth:

> And all King Solomon's drinking vessels were of gold, and all the vessels of the house of the forest of Lebanon were of pure gold; none were of silver: it was not considered as anything in the days of Solomon.   (1 Kings 10:21)

Can you believe it! Solomon had drinking chalices of gold only. He would not take a drink of water from a silver cup, for silver was not considered as anything in that day.

This incredible wealth was in direct disobedience to God. God had allowed in His law for the normal blessings which would accrue to a king, but He had specifically warned against personally motivated accumulation of riches:

> When thou art come unto the land which the Lord thy God giveth thee, and shalt possess it and shalt dwell therein, and shalt say, I will set a king over me . . . He shall *not* multiply horses *to* himself . . . neither shall he multiply wives to himself . . . neither shall he greatly multiply to himself silver and gold.
> (Deuteronomy 17:14-17)

It is obvious that Solomon violated all of these prohibitions. His own words document the story of his quest after riches. I cannot certify the time in Solomon's life when these words were written, but *they are his* words, and they do tell the story of his greedy heart:

> I said in mine heart, go to now, I will prove thee with mirth, therefore enjoy pleasure . . . I made me great works: I builded me houses; I planted me vineyards: I made me gardens and orchards, and planted trees in them of all kinds of fruits: I made me pools of water, to water therewith the wood that bringeth forth trees: I got me servants and maidens, and had servants born in my house; also I had great possessions of great and small cattle above all that were in Jerusalem before me: I gathered me also silver and gold, and the peculiar treasure of kings and of the provinces. I got me men singers and women singers and the delights of the sons of men, as musical instruments, and that of all sorts. So I was great, and increased more than all that were before me in Jerusalem: also my wisdom remained with me. And whatsoever mine eyes desired I kept not from them, I withheld not my heart from any joy.(Ecclesiastes 2:1-10)

Even the wealth that David provided for the building of Solomon's temple speedily disappeared under Solomon's lavish spending, and in the end, the people had to pay heavily by taxation and poverty for his magnificent whims.

Solomon set his heart upon wealth, and this is the first reason for his downfall. We come secondly to this:

HE HAD AN INCREDIBLE APPETITE FOR WOMEN

The first words of 1 Kings 11 are sad words for those of us who love Solomon:

> But King Solomon loved many strange women . . . of the nations concerning which the Lord said unto the children of Israel, ye shall not go in to them, neither shall they come in unto you: for surely they will turn away your heart after their gods: *Solomon clave unto these in love.*
>
> And he had seven hundred wives, princesses, and three hundred concubines: and his wives turned away his heart.
>
> (1 Kings 11:1-3)

Here is "the wisest man who ever lived" trying to keep one thousand women happy. In doing so, he violated his own instruction and disobeyed his own commands. The words of warning, which he passed on in his proverbs, became the indictment of his own soul.

> And why wilt thou, my Son, be ravished with a strange woman, and embrace the bosom of a stranger? For the ways of man are before the eyes of the Lord, and he pondereth all his goings. His own iniquities shall take the wicked himself, and he shall be holden with the cords of his sins. He shall die without instruction; and in the greatness of his folly he shall go astray.
> (Proverbs 5:20-23)

At first his sin was immorality and sensuality, but in the end, it became gross idolatry. His many wives turned away his heart after other gods'' (1 Kings 11:3, 4).

It was his *heart* that became the problem. When Jehovah appeared before Solomon the second time at the completion of the temple, He instructed him to walk before God as his father David had walked, *in integrity of heart . . .* (1 Kings 9:4). In his sin, *"His heart was not perfect with the Lord his God*, as was the heart of David his father (1 Kings 11:4).

The result of Solomon's immorality and idolatry is clearly listed for us in the last part of 1 Kings 11:

> And the Lord was angry with Solomon, because his heart was turned away from the Lord God of Israel, which had appeared unto him twice. And had commanded him concerning this thing, that he should not go after other gods: but he kept not that which the Lord commanded. Wherefore the Lord said unto Solomon, forasmuch as this is done of thee, and thou hast not kept my covenant and my statutes, which I have commanded thee, I will surely rend the kingdom from thee, and will give it to thy servants. (1 Kings 11:9-11)

The rest of I Kings 11 is the record of what happened to Solomon, the man of great privilege and opportunity, when he turned his back upon God.

1. King Hadad of the Edomites became a thorn in Solomon's side for the rest of his reign (vv. 14-22).
2. A band of guerrilla soldiers led by Rezon became Solomon's adversaries all the rest of his days (vv. 23-25).
3. Jereboam, the son of one of Solomon's servants, led a revolt against Solomon's administration and plagued him until Solomon banished him to Egypt (vv. 26-43).

The shipwreck of Solomon was surely one of the most terrible tragedies in all the world. For if ever there was a shining type of Christ in the Old Testament, it was Solomon. Everyday sensuality made him, at the end of his life, nothing more than a castaway. His wisdom failed to teach him self-control. The only legacy which he left was a son who was more foolish than he was. Solomon died in his early sixties knowing that the great kingdom he had built would be taken from him and broken in two.

As I have pondered the life and leadership of Solomon, four important lessons have emerged.

INADEQUATE BARRIERS TO SIN

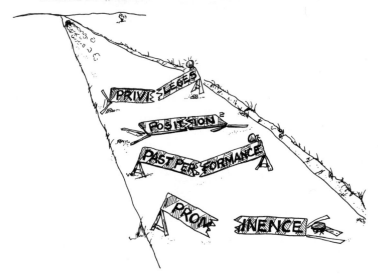

HIS PROMINENCE DID NOT KEEP HIM FROM SIN.

Thousands of men that we all know have been wrecked, going up the hill of what they considered the improbable and impossible temptation. The things happen to them that could never happen, and men all around them say, "Who would have thought it? Why, that's the last person I would ever have supposed would have fallen into such a trap."

The great doers of evil in history have all been men who thought they could never do it! When Napoleon was a youth, he wrote an essay for the Lions Academy on the dangers of ambition. When Nero was asked to sign his first death warrant, he exclaimed, "Would that this hand had never learned to write." The thing unthought often becomes the deed accomplished.

If we could have stood with David after he had killed Goliath, in the moment of his great victory, and would have said to him, "David, this is a glorious night for you, but within a few short years, you will commit adultery and murder," he would have looked at us in astonishment.

If we had been present on that night when Peter boasted of his fidelity to Jesus, and we had told Peter that before the wine was dry upon his lips he would deny his Lord with an oath, Peter would have said, "Never."

If we had been present on the night when Solomon had his wonderful dream and God granted his request for wisdom, and we had warned that great king that before his reign was over he would be on his knees worshipping a foreign god in idolatry, Solomon would have pushed us away as lunatics.

But you see, wisdom does not automatically *immunize* anyone from the sickness of sin.

HIS PAST PERFORMANCE DID NOT KEEP HIM FROM SIN.

Solomon committed these sins after he had a lifetime of acceptable performance for God. The Bible spells it out clearly, "For it came to pass, when Solomon was old, that his wives turned away his heart after other gods . . ." (1 Kings 11:4). There is no fool like an old fool . . . here was Solomon pushing sixty and chasing a thousand women.

They say that when William Jennings Bryan went to call on the father of his prospective wife to seek her hand in marriage, knowing the strong religious feelings of this man, Bryan hoped to strengthen his case by using a quotation from the Bible. He quoted the Proverb that says, "Whoso findeth a wife, findeth a good thing" (Proverbs 18:22). But to his surprise, the father replied with a citation from Paul that, "He that giveth her in marriage doeth well; but he that giveth her not in marriage doeth better" (1 Corinthians 7:38).

The young suitor was, for a minute, confused and then with a happy inspiration, replied while Paul had no wives, Solomon had seven hundred and, therefore, ought to be better qualified to judge the reality of marriage!

We chuckle at that, but we know in our hearts that it is no laughing matter. In his old age, he turned away from God. I am reminded, by this episode in Solomon's life, that no one is ever too old to bring sorrow and shame to God. Someone has written that we are not safe until we drag our tired heels through the pearly gates.

We sometimes hear it said about certain men that if only they had died at this point or at that point in their great career, it would have been better for their fame. If Benedict Arnold had died at Saratoga or Quebec, we would think differently about him today. If David had died when he returned the ark to Jerusalem, he would have been as clean as Joseph. If Solomon had died when the temple was finished . . . but he did not, and he failed God in his old age.

You can never tell by the brightness of the dawn or the noonday how the evening of the day will be. The brightest sun may go down in a dark and cloudy sky.

HIS POSITION DID NOT KEEP HIM FROM SIN.

What was Solomon's position? There was none higher in all the land. He was the king. Here was the authority doing that which he should have been forbidding his subjects to do. Here was the leader being led away from God. Here was David's son forsaking David's God. Here was the wisest man who ever lived acting the fool.

Preachers, deacons, teachers, and workers in the church are all alike in their susceptibility to the snare of sin.

HIS PRIVILEGES DID NOT KEEP HIM FROM SIN.

1 Kings 11:9 tells of the anger of the Lord with Solomon and then, almost as an addendum, adds this phrase, ". . . the Lord God of Israel, who had appeared unto him twice." Solomon had been privileged during his lifetime to talk with the God of Israel, in person, on two different occasions.

He had been singled out by the Lord for what looks, from the human perspective, like "special" treatment. Yet even this did not prevent his collapse. Nor will the special privileges accorded to us make the final difference. Good family background, good education, good religious instruction, good companions . . . all of these are helpful, but none of them alone, nor all of them together, are enough to prevent our defection.

HOW DID IT HAPPEN?

I wondered as I read Solomon's life story just where it was in his life that he began to give ground to the enemy. Solomon did not become an idolator overnight. He did not become a polygamist in a day. In the language of today, his demise was a gradual process. It was not a blowout . . . it was a slow leak.

Somewhere along the way, Solomon's quest for wealth began to replace his quest for the Word of God. One day his appetite for women replaced his appetite for God. Solomon's desire for success and accomplishment began to push the important spiritual things out of his life.

Listen to the parable of the forest. The trees of the forest held a solemn meeting to discuss the wrongs that were being done by the little instrument called the ax. They insisted that this instrument had no power of its own without a handle. Obviously, the handle had to come from the wood of the forest. So the forest agreed together that no tree should be allowed to furnish any ax with a handle on the penalty that it would be cut down to its roots.

The ax visited the forest to seek a handle. He journeyed through the forest begging from the ash tree and the cedar tree and the oak tree and the willow tree and the poplar tree; and everywhere he got a stern denial. No one would fill his request.

Not to be denied, he came again another day. And this time he said, "I desire just a small indulgence. Just a small chip . . . just a small twig that I can fasten on my axhead to cut down the briars and the bushes that are such a plague to all of you trees in the forest." Since no tree could come up with a good reason for denying that request, the forest agreed to give the axhead a fragment of wood which a storm had broken from a sapling . . . a mere little stick.

But the ax made a small handle from that twig, and severed a branch from a giant oak tree. Then the ax fitted himself with a bigger handle and down came the elms, down came the cedars, down came the poplar trees. The time for defense was passed, and the forest had surrendered.

If you would ask the fallen when it happened, they would tell you the time when it became known. But if the truth were revealed, you would trace their fall to some moment in the distant past when they let their guard down, for just a moment, and allowed the enemy to get his foot in the door.

Solomon was the wisest man who ever lived, but he was not wise enough to evaluate the power of small concessions.

Many years ago in the museums of our land, two paintings hung side by side, and circulated together to all the famous halls of art. The two pictures were two different views of Rome. The first pictured the glory days of Rome, *The Pax Romana*, when Rome ruled the world. The other showed Rome after it had been conquered. It portrayed graphically the defeat, ruin, and debris of a conquered people. Those who visited the museum stood in wonder before the stark contrast of the two scenes.

If we had the artist's gift, we could illustrate the life of Solomon in a similar fashion. The first view would be of the gold age of Hebrew history, when Solomon reigned in all of his glory and splendor . . . wealth was on every hand, the land was at peace with her enemies, and Solomon's temple was finished. The people worshipped God. It was a glory day for Israel.

The second picture would be a view of Israel at the end of Solomon's life; his kingdom at the point of division, and he, a sixty-year-old defeated and discouraged man.

Looking at Solomon from our perspective, he is a disappointing figure in Hebrew history. Think of the advantages he began with:

* The undisputed possession of David's throne.
* The unbelievable wealth inherited from his father.
* The unparalleled mental abilities divinely imparted to him.
* The unconditional love and admiration of his people.

Solomon's start in life was like the beginning of a cloudless day. He might have known good weather all through life, but he wandered into God-forbidden paths, and the magnificent beginning was turned into a miserable ending. The man who penned and preached a thousand wise sayings failed to practice the wisdom he taught.

His failure calls to mind the prayer of another Old Testament figure who also prayed for the blessing of God upon his life. There is one small addition to his prayer, however, that Solomon should have included in his request:

> And Jabez was more honorable than his brethren . . . And Jabez called on the God of Israel, saying, Oh that thou wouldest bless me inded, and enlarge my coast, *and that thine hand might be with me, and that thou wouldest keep me from evil*, that it may not grieve me! And God granted him that which he requested.
>
> (1 Chronicles 4:9-10)

God granted Jabez the blessing he sought after, and he also honored his request for protection from evil. How foolish to pray for one without the other.

8

Wisdom For A Lifetime

Solomon was wise for a time but failed in the end. David had his moments of glory, but his life was checkered with problems. Moses was a great man, but he gave in to the flesh. But "Daniel continued even unto the first year of King Cyrus" (Daniel 1:21).

Dr. Wilbur Smith captures the magnitude of this thought:

> It is generally considered that of all men who ever lived, Solomon was the wisest. But we should not forget that twice as many different words in the original text are used to describe and define the learning of the prophet of Babylon as are found necessary to particularize the wisdom of Solomon hundreds of years before. Furthermore, the wisdom of Solomon turned to folly, and he became involved in the greatest of sins; that of Daniel kept him holy and loyal to God through all of the challenges of his great career.[1]

Daniel rose from his humble position as a slave in Babylon to one promotion after another. Ultimately, he became the ruler of the province of Babylon. He lived through all the troubles of his nation. In the midst of whirling intrigues, envies, plots, the king's insanity, and the actual destruction of Babylon, Daniel stood firm like a pillar.

When Daniel was first brought to Babylon, the prince of the eunuchs gave him the name Belteshazzar which means, "he whom Bel favors." But Daniel enjoyed the favor of God, not Bel.

Nebuchadnezzar loaded Daniel with gifts and honors. The king's grandson, Belshazzar made Daniel the third ruler in the kingdom. Darius, the Median king, preferred Daniel "above the presidents and princes . . . because an excellent spirit was in him; and the king (Darius) thought to set him over the whole realm" (Daniel 6:3).

After Daniel's experience in the lion's den is recorded in Daniel 6, this postscript is added: "So this Daniel prospered in the reign of Darius and in the reign of Cyrus the Persian'' (Daniel 6:28).

What other man can you mention who filled with distinction the position of prime minister under five kings, some of whom were of different dynasties?

There's no question about it, the distinction of Daniel's life was this . . . *He continued.*

He was in the public eye all of his life, but he continued.

He was in the court from his youth up, but he continued.

He lived in an utterly pagan culture, but he continued.

A lasting tribute to the wisdom of Daniel is provided by his contemporary, Ezekiel. On three separate occasions, Ezekiel links Daniel with Noah and Job.

> The word of the Lord came again to me saying, Son of Man, when the land sinneth against me by trespassing grievously, then will I stretch out mine hand upon it . . . Though these three men, Noah, Daniel, and Job were in it, they should deliver but their own souls by their righteousness, said the Lord.
>
> (Ezekiel 14:12-14)

On another occasion in the book of Ezekiel, God speaks to the prince of Tyre. In this particular instance, he addresses Lucifer, the Son of the Morning, who came to be Satan, our great enemy. When God wished to describe his wisdom He said, ''Behold, thou art wiser than Daniel'' (Ezekiel 28:3). We would expect Solomon to be the example, but God chose Daniel instead. This certainly demonstrates how God appreciated the wisdom of Daniel.

When the presidents and the princes, who served under Darius the Mede, tried to find some occasion to accuse Daniel, we are told that, ''They could find none occasion nor fault, forasmuch as he was faithful, neither was there any error or fault found in him'' (Daniel 6:4). Daniel, like Joseph and Jonathan, lived in such a way that no evil word is recorded of him in the entire Bible.

Daniel's life and his wisdom are not unique because of the high peaks of performance but because of the high plane of ministry. No wonder he is described on three different occasions as ''the man greatly beloved'' (Daniel 9:23; 10:11; 10:19). Only our Lord shares that title with Daniel, and I believe Daniel was beloved both of God and by his fellow man.

What was the secret of Daniel's lasting impact and success?

J. C. Ryle, the nineteenth century bishop of Liverpool, may have given us the answer. He wrote:

> I have read the lives of many eminent Christians who have been on earth since the Bible days. Some of them I see were rich, some were poor. Some were learned, some unlearned. Some of them were Episcopalians, and some Christians of other denominations. Some were Calvinists, and some Armenians. Some have loved to use a liturgy, and some chose to use none. But one thing I see they all had in common. They all have been men of prayer.[2]

Daniel's wisdom came from God's Word, but the longevity of that wisdom was related to his personal walk with the Lord. He prayed God's Word into his life until he lived in the very presence of God everyday. It mattered little who was on the throne of the earthly kingdom. Daniel knew the heavenly King and spent time in His presence each day. Daniel's favorite name for God was "The God of Heaven." Because of his consistent prayer life, he was able to bring heaven to bear upon earth.

Several characteristics mark the prayer life of Daniel and account for the continual wisdom with which he was blessed.

DANIEL'S PRAYER LIFE WAS MARKED BY CONSISTENCY.

Daniel's prayer habit was born out in the story of the lion's den recorded in Daniel chapter 6:

> Now when Daniel knew that the writing was signed, he went into his house, and his windows being open in his chamber toward Jerusalem, he kneeled upon his knees three times a day, and prayed, and gave thanks before his God, as he did aforetime. (Daniel 6:10)

The last phrase of this verse is the important truth. Daniel prayed three times a day as he was accustomed to doing. In other words, his habit in prayer involved a special time of protracted prayer, morning, noon, and at night.

Leon Wood comments on this part of Daniel's daily walk with God:

> To have maintained such a demanding prayer schedule as this . . . required great discipline of life. In his position as president, Daniel carried heavy responsibility, with much work to

DANIEL'S PRAYER SECRETS

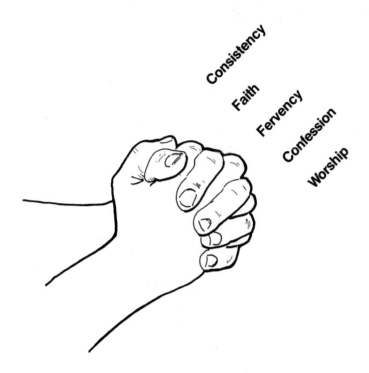

Consistency

Faith

Fervency

Confession

Worship

do. Under such demands the temptation to neglect this sort of prayer program was no doubt strong, especially since he had to return home each noon for the purpose, while keeping on also with the morning and evening occasions. But Daniel had maintained it, apparently recognizing the priority of this contract with God.[3]

We who would know the wisdom of God are instructed to do as Daniel did:

And he spake a parable unto them to this end, that *men ought always to pray*, and not to faint.   (Luke 18:1)

These *all continued* with one accord in prayer and supplication, with the women, and Mary the mother of Jesus, and with his brethren.   (Acts 1:14)

They *continued steadfastly* in the apostles' doctrine and fellowship and in breaking of bread, *and in prayers.*(Acts 2:42)

We will give ourselves *continually to prayer.*   (Acts 6:4)

Rejoicing in hope; patient in tribulation; *continuing instant in prayer.*   (Romans 12:12)

Pray without ceasing.   (1 Thessalonians 5:17)

Continue in prayer, and watch in the same with thanksgiving.
(Colossians 4:2)

DANIEL'S PRAYER LIFE WAS MARKED BY FAITH.

When Daniel prayed, he prayed toward Jerusalem. This practice demonstrated his faith in God's ability to hear and answer. The background of this custom is given in a prayer of Solomon recorded in 1 Kings 8:46-52:

> If they sin against thee, (for there is no man that sinneth not), and thou be angry with them, and deliver them to the enemy, so that they carry them away captives unto the land of the enemy, far and near. Yet if they shall bethink themselves in the land whither they were carried captives, and repent, and make supplication unto thee in the land of them that carried them captives, saying, We have sinned, and have done perversely, we have committed wickedness; And so return unto thee with all their heart, and with all their soul, in the land of their enemies, which led them away captive, *and pray unto thee toward* their land, which thou gavest unto their fathers, the city which thou hast chosen, and the house which I have built for thy name: Then hear thou their prayer and their supplication in heaven thy dwelling place, and maintain their cause.
> (1 Kings 8:46-49)

When Daniel prayed toward Jerusalem, he prayed in faith. He believed God for the end of the captivity. Daniel's greatest weapon was his faith. An unknown author sees faith as central too:

> When faith in God goes,
>   Man the thinker loses his greatest thought.
> When faith in God goes,
>   Man the worker loses his greatest motive.
> When faith in God goes,
>   Man the sufferer loses his securest refuge.

> When faith in God goes,
> > Man the lover loses his fairest vision.
> When faith in God goes,
> > Man the mortal loses his only hope.

DANIEL'S PRAYER LIFE WAS MARKED BY FERVENCY.

In the New Testament we are reminded by James that "The effectual fervent prayer of a righteous man availeth much" (James 5:16). When Daniel prayed, he prayed fervently. His prayer to God during captivity is described as "prayer and supplications, with fasting, and sackcloth and ashes" (Daniel 9:2).

In the Bible, fervency in prayer was often accompanied by outward expressions such as smiting the breast, tearing one's garments, sitting in ashes or putting them on the head. The most common expression of fervency was fasting.

We seem to have forgotten the act of fasting, but a brief look back through history reveals a long line of men and women who sought the Lord earnestly and fasted. Jesus, the Apostle Paul, the early church leaders, Isaiah, Daniel, Esther, David, Hannah, Elijah, Ezra, Nehemiah, and Zechariah are among the more notable Bible characters who fasted.

From a more recent period of history, we could add Martin Luther, John Calvin, John Knox, John Wesley, David Brainerd, George Mueller, Rees Howells, and many others. Though fasting is not the only expression of fervency, it is certainly one way to express our intense desire in prayer.

As he reviewed the lives of those who fasted, Andrew Murray wrote:

> Learn from these men that the work which the Holy Spirit commands must call us to new fasting and prayer, to new separation from the spirit and pleasures of the world, to new consecration to God and His fellowship. These men gave themselves up to fasting and prayer, and if in all our ordinary Christian work there were more prayer, there would be more blessing in our inner life.

I have always liked what Paul wrote about his friend Epaphras. He described him as "a servant of Christ . . . always laboring fervently for you in prayers that ye may stand perfect and complete in all the will of God" (Colossians 4:12).

As we look around today, it appears that we have lost much of the fervency in our Christian experience. Edgar Young Mullens pictures our plight:

> A little monkey got loose from the organ grinder in the cold wintertime, and the little thing, freezing to death, jumped upon the windowsill of a house. As he looked through the window, he saw a roaring fire. As quickly as possible, he found a way into the room, and he sat there with his little paws raised to the fire and froze to death, because it was a painted fire on a painted screen.[4]

For many of us, our fervency in prayer is described well as "a painted fire on a painted screen."

Usually our fervency in prayer is related to the *need* we sense of God. I think that was what Sam Walter Foss was trying to get across when he wrote this somewhat humorous poem on prayer:

> The proper way for a man to pray
> Said Deacon Lemuel Keyes,
> And the only proper attitude
> Is down upon his knees.
>
> No, I should say the way to pray
> Said Reverend Doctor Wise,
> Is standing straight with outstretched arms
> And rapt and upturned eyes.
>
> Oh, no, no, no, no said Elmer Slow,
> Such posture is too proud.
> A man should pray with eyes fast closed,
> And head contritely bowed.
>
> It seems to me his hands should be
> Austerely clasped in front
> With both thumbs pointing toward the ground
> Said Reverend Doctor Blunt.
>
> Last year, I fell in Hidgekin's well,
> Head first said Cyrus Brown,
> With both my heels a stickin' up
> And my head apointin' down.
>
> And I made a prayer right then and there,
> The best prayer I ever said,
> The prayingest prayer I ever prayed,
> A standin' on my head.[5]

It isn't our position; it is our fervency that God wants. "The effective fervent prayer of a righteous man availeth much" (James 5:16).

DANIEL'S PRAYER LIFE WAS MARKED BY CONFESSION.

Toward the end of the seventy years of captivity through which Daniel lived, he began to understand, through the reading of Jeremiah's prophecy, that God's time for the end of captivity had arrived. He didn't know the exact time, but he knew that Jeremiah's words were about to be fulfilled.

"For thus saith the Lord, that after seventy years be accomplished at Babylon, I will visit you, and perform my good word toward you, in causing you to return to this place" (Jeremiah 29:10).

When Daniel knew what God was about to do, he began to pray and confess his sins and the sins of his people:

> And I set my face unto the Lord God, to seek by prayer and supplications, with fasting and sackcloth, and ashes: And I prayed unto the Lord my God, and made my confession.
>
> (Daniel 9:2-3)

At first notice, Daniel's action seems contradictory. This is that Daniel about whom no evil word is written in the Scriptures. This is that Daniel who was closely scrutinized and investigated by the leader of Babylon:

> Then the presidents and princes sought to find occasion against Daniel concerning the kingdom; but they could find none occasion nor fault; forasmuch as he was faithful, neither was there any error or fault found in him.   (Daniel 6:4)

When Daniel brought his confession to God, he spoke of sin, iniquity, doing wickedly, rebelling, acting perversely and defying authority. Though he had not personally been involved in these activities, he nonetheless identified himself with his people. "*We* ignored your spokesmen. *We* are shame-faced. *We* refused to obey." Daniel saw himself as a part of the whole. He spoke of *"my* sin and the sin of *my people"* (Daniel 9:20).

Daniel teaches us that when God is at work in a life, repentance and confession become the norm. The New Testament word for confess means "to agree with God about my sin." It also means "to admit my guilt." Confession simply stated is the act of declared admission.

Confession is the heartfelt recognition of what we are. It is important to God because it indicates that we take seriously our mistakes and failures. God does not ask us to confess our sins because he needs to know that we have sinned, but because He knows that we need to acknowledge our sin.

The secret to Daniel's longevity in the service of God is found right here. He walked humbly before his God and understood the importance of confession. And confession, *true* confession is a painful experience. The moment we admit that a particular act displeases God, we recognize the responsibility to change it, and immediately an inner battle of the will begins to take place.

E. M. Blaiklock explains:

> This period of our devotions must contain a moment of pain. It is not God's intention that should writhe under it or linger in it. But specific and sincere confession of our own is no joyous exercise and self-contempt, however salutary, is not pleasant. But let evil in conduct, thought, or motive be brought into the open, fully, without excuse, and under proper names. It is no use, after all, to pose before god.[6]

Daniel's confession is the true indication of his character. The more devout one's soul is . . . the deeper one's love for God is. The higher one's standard of holiness is . . . the truer one's commitment to Christ, and the greater will be one's sense of his own sinfulness.

DANIEL'S PRAYER LIFE WAS MARKED BY WORSHIP

Daniel's prayer of confession explodes into praise. He praises God for His greatness and His majesty. He extols the mercy, righteousness, faithfulness, and holiness of his God.

Paul Billheimer writes:

> Praise is the most useful occupation and activity in enabling God to realize the supreme goal of the universe, that of bringing many sons into glory. If we want to get in good with God, he said, just brag on His Son.[7]

When Jesus was teaching His disciples to pray, He taught them to begin with praise, "Our Father which art in heaven, hallowed by Thy name" (Matthew 6:9).

But He also taught us to end our prayers with praise, "For thine is the kingdom, and the power, and the glory, forever. Amen" (Matt. 6:13).

Quoting Billheimer again:

> It (praise) is the summum bonum, the greatest good, the highest joy, the most exquisite delight, the supreme rapture, the most ravishing transport of the human spirit. Just as antagonism, hostility, and cursing against God exercises and strengthens all that is most abominable, diabolical and base in the human spirit, so worship and praise of the infinitely loving, lovely God exercises, reinforces, and strengthens all that is most sublime, transcendent, and divine in the inner being. Thus, as one worships and praises God, he is continually transformed step by step, from glory to glory into the image of the infinitely happy God.[8]

I believe Daniel's worship and praise of God made it possible for him to endure all those difficult years. One of the greatest values of praise is this: It decentralizes self. The worship and praise of God demands a shift of center from self to God. It would have been easy for Daniel to have become occupied with his own wisdom and his own problems. But one cannot praise God without relinquishing occupation with self. Praise produces forgetfulness of self.

These words poetically describe the value of such praying:

> Lord, what a change within us one short hour
> Spent in Thy presence will avail to make!
> What heavy burdens from our bosoms take!
> What parched grounds refresh as with a shower!
> We kneel, and all around us seems to lower;
> We rise, and all, the distant and the near,
> Stands forth in sunny outline, brave and clear;
> We kneel, how weak; we rise, how full of power!
> Why, therefore, should we do ourselves this wrong,
> Or others—that we are not always strong—
> That we are sometimes overborne with care—
> That we should ever weak or heartless be,
> Anxious or troubled—when with us in prayer,
> And joy and strength and courage are with Thee?

Daniel's entire prayer was in order that the name of the Lord might be glorified. He was jealous for the reputation of God. As his prayer concludes in Daniel 9, God is the prominent one in the prayer. Note the pronouns and other references to God:

O Lord, according to all *thy righteousness*, I beseech thee, let thine anger and thy fury be turned away from *thy* city Jerusalem, *thy* holy mountain . . .

. . . cause *thy* face to shine upon *thy* sanctuary that is desolate, *for the Lord's* sake.

O my God, incline thine ear, and hear; open thine eyes, and behold our desolations, and the city which is called by *thy* name: for we do not present our supplications before thee for our righteousnesses, but for thy great mercies.

O Lord, hear; O Lord, forgive; O Lord, hearken and do; defer not *for thine own sake*, O my God: for thy city and thy people are called by thy name.   (Daniel 9:16-19)

Daniel prayed consistently and fervently, and his prayers were mixed with faith, confession, and worship. God blessed Daniel because of his praying and he walked in God's wisdom for over seventy years.

As I have studied this man's life, I have been tempted to feel that he is out of my reach. No one could live so consistently and walk so intimately with the Lord. How can I relate to such perfection? These words from Alexander Whyte encourage me to believe God for such a lifestyle today:

The prophet Daniel became a great proficient in the penitential and in intercessary prayer also as the years went on. And he came to that great proficiency just as a great proficiency is come to in any other science or art; that is to say, by constant, and unremitting, and enterprising practice. Lord, teach us to pray, said a disciple on one occasion to our Lord. But not even our Lord with all His willingness, and with all His ability, can teach any of us off-hand to pray. Every man must teach himself, every day he lives, this most personal, most secret, and most experimental of all the arts.

Every man must find out the best ways of prayer for himself. There is no royal road; there is no short or easy road to proficiency in prayer. It is like all the other arts that you have ever mastered; it must be early begun and assiduously practiced, else you will be a bungler at it all your days. You must also have special and extraordinary seasons of prayer, as Daniel had, over and above his daily habit of prayer, special and extraordinary, original and unparalleled seasons of prayer, when you literally do nothing else day nor night but pray. You must pray in your very dream, till you come at last to live and move, and have your whole being in prayer.[10]

NOTES

1. Oswald Sanders, *Robust In Faith* (Chicago: Moody Press, 1965), p. 165.
2. J. C. Ryle, *A Call To Prayer* (Grand Rapids: Baker Book House, 1976), pp. 14-15.
3. Leon Wood, *A Commentary On Daniel* (Grand Rapids: Zondervan Pub., 1973), p. 103.
4. Edgar Young Mullens, Quoted by W. A. Criswell in a taped message entitled, "The Church in the City," Waco, Texas: Word Records.
5. Sam Walter Foss, "Hidgekin's Well" in *Source book of Poetry*, ed. Al Bryant (Grand Rapids: Zondervan Pub., 1968).
6. E. M. Blaiklock, *The Positive Power of Prayer* (Glendale: Regal Books, 1974), p. 43.
7. Paul Billheimer, *Destined For The Throne* (Fort Washington: Christian Literature Crusade, 1976), p. 117.
8. Ibid, pp. 116-117.
9. Richard Chenevix Trench, "An Hour With Thee" in *Source book of Poetry*, p. 132.
10. Alexander Whyte, "Daniel," *Bible Characters—The Old Testament* (Grand Rapids: Zondervan, 1964), pp. 168-172.

How To Pray For Wisdom

The big animals and the little animals were engaged in a championship football game. Because of their size, the big animals were just killing the little animals. In fact, the score at the end of the first half was 72-0 in favor of the elephants, giraffes, lions, and friends.

During the intermission, there was a serious discussion in the little animal's locker room, and as the half-time concluded, believe it or not, the underdogs ran out on the field ready to play the second half.

The big animals received the kickoff and the ball was taken out to the twenty-yard line after it was booted into the end zone. On their first play from scrimmage, the big animals ran the elephant around the right end. Smash! He was tackled at the line of scrimmage. Rather stunned, since they had scored on every play in the first half, the monsters from the zoo decided to run a screen pass to the giraffe around the left end. Once again, the play was stopped for no gain.

After a brief discussion in the huddle, they decided it was time to use their secret weapon. "We'll give the ball to the zebra up the middle." This time there was a huge pile-up and when the dust had settled, the zebra had been stopped five yards behind the line of scrimmage.

"Time out!" called the captain.

The big animals gathered on one side and the little animals huddled around their startled captain on the other side.

"Who stopped the elephant going around the right end?" asked the leader of the little animals.

"I did," said the centipede.

"And who hit the giraffe going around the left end?" he asked again.

"I did," admitted the centipede.

"And who tackled the zebra for a five yard loss?" quizzed the captain. Once again the centipede spoke, "I did, sir."

"Good night, man," said the leader, "where were you in the first half?"

"I was in the locker room, sir, getting my ankles taped."

My four-year-old son, Danny, thinks that's the neatest story he ever heard. Whenever anyone tells a joke, Danny always says, "Tell them about the animals, Daddy." So, I guess I've told that rather corny, little anecdote several dozen times.

Apart from making an old athlete glad that he has only two ankles to tape instead of a hundred, each time I tell that story I am reminded of the simple lesson it illustrates . . . *Proper preparation is absolutely essential for successful performance.*

Athletes spend hours of practice preparing for the two hours of competition. Actors and actresses invest months of memorization and rehearsal for a one-hour television drama. Businessmen I know have spent years getting into position for a major acquisition that has been signed, sealed, and delivered in a matter of minutes. The actual performance is the top of the iceberg. Beneath the surface is the magnitude of energy and hours unnoticed by the spectator but absolutely essential to success.

I fear that some of us view the "successful" Christians we know with a kind of simple naivete. I have heard them explained this way, "They just have it all together . . . they just always seem to do the right thing."

I have been learning that the outwardly, and genuinely wise and successful Christians I know can only be explained in terms of the hidden portion of their lives. As I listen carefully and observe closely, I discover that behind the outward facade of wisdom is the secret and inward prayer life of the man.

As always, if we are anxious to know the truth, God has a word for us. That word is the subject of the instruction given by James to a group of tired and persecuted Jews who were experiencing difficulties you and I will probably never encounter.

"If any of you lack wisdom, let him ask of God" (James 5:5). The need is wisdom; the preparation is *prayer*. J. B. Phillips has translated this phrase, "If any of you does not know how to meet any particular problem, let him ask of God."

This instruction concerning wisdom is given by James in a context which focuses on the problems and difficulties of life. James speaks of the "various trials" we face and of the "testing of our faith." He shocks us by saying that we are to face these times with joy.

How can anybody be expected to go through life smiling at his setbacks and laughing at his losses? How can anybody be joyous when the circumstances of his life dictate depression?

James teaches that the trials and testings and losses and discouragements of life are tests that God uses to make us mature and complete in Him. All of us agree with the goal God has in mind, but the method He chooses to achieve His goal is often more than we can handle. Do I want to be mature? Certainly! Do I want "various trials and testings?" Are you kidding?

God says that these testings will come without our permission. No vote is taken! *But* when they do come, we may have God's perspective on these things if we will prepare ahead of time! The trials and testings will come, *but* if we lack wisdom (God's perspective), we are to ask of God.

A young couple from Yokohama, Japan, wrote a letter to their family during the Christmas season of 1958. The letter told of the tragic loss of their only son, who had just died of leukemia. The child's body had been buried far from their homeland. Therefore these parents were robbed of the loving comfort of their family and close relatives to help them through this time of trial.

How could this possibly be explained in terms of God? Why would God take all that they had left when they had given up all to serve Him in a foreign land?

Their letter spoke of their great loss, and it was filled with sadness. Yet, two sentences stood out to tell of their wholeness and maturity as Christians. The first sentence said, "At a time when the empty hours would echo with little memories, we find the pressures of work a welcome problem." All sufferers understand this truth!

The second sentence was even more meaningful. "We will need the wisdom of God to understand how this even fits into His plan for our lives."

That is really what wisdom is all about . . . facing life's situations with the perspective of God's wisdom.

Here, then, is James' three-step formula for acquiring God's wisdom in your life.

PRESCRIPTION FOR PRAYER

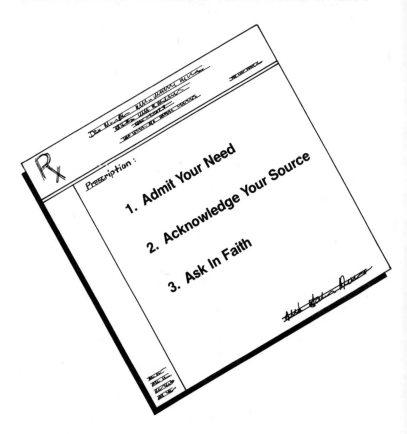

1. ADMIT YOUR NEED

"If any of you *lack* wisdom, let him ask of God." Only as we see our own need is God able to meet that need. When we are satisfied with our own perspective, we will never have the joy of knowing life as God longs for us to know it.

If we are humbly willing to admit our lack of wisdom, God is ready to penetrate the fog of our sorrow and suffering and put our testings to use. He will help us to see these difficulties, not as enemies, but as friends.

A missionary I know wrote home from the field not long ago and asked her friends to pray for her during a time of severe testing in her family. She did not ask them to pray for the testing to go away, or for it necessarily to get better. But, she asked that they would pray that she would not miss the opportunity that God had for her in the midst of this difficulty.

When God answered her prayer, she became the master of her circumstances instead of the servant of them.

It has been my experience, as a pastor, that there are only two alternatives to the wisdom of God in the midst of difficulty. If we refuse to admit our need and seek God's wisdom, we become very susceptible to the philosophy of *fatalism*. "Whatever will be, will be. . . ." "What difference does it make?" "Who cares, anyway?" The end of fatalism is despair and despair has pointed a gun at the head of many a troubled man.

The other alternative to God's wisdom in the midst of difficulty is the attitude of bitterness. I have watched bitterness literally destroy some of my Christian brothers and sisters simply because they refused to let go of their own perspective on their problems.

Somewhere in my reading, I came across this succinct statement of our predicament, *Unless there is within us, that which is above us, we will soon yield to that which is around us.*

2. ACKNOWLEDGE YOUR SOURCE

"If any of you lack wisdom let him ask of God that giveth to all men liberally" (James 1:5). Once we admit our need, we are to turn away from our emptiness and focus on His fullness.

True wisdom is to be found in God alone, for "Every good gift and every perfect gift is from above, and cometh down from the father of lights, with whom is no variableness, neither shadow of turning" (James 1:17).

By His wisdom, God numbered the clouds (Job 38:37). By His wisdom, ". . . He hath established the world . . . and stretched out the heavens by His discretion" (Jeremiah 10:12).

"With Him is wisdom and strength; he hath counsel and understanding" (Job 12:13).

"For the Lord giveth wisdom: out of His mouth cometh knowledge and understanding" (Proverbs 2:6).

"Whence then cometh wisdom? And where is the place of understanding? God understandeth its way, and knoweth the place of it" (Job 28:20, 23).

"For God giveth to a man that is good in his sight wisdom, and knowledge, and joy" (Ecclesiastes 2:26).

"Blessed be the name of God forever and ever, for wisdom and might are his" (Daniel 2:20).

When I recognize that God by His wisdom established the earth, I realize at once that He is able to decipher the difficulties in my life. Three wonderful truths about God help me to believe that what God is able to do, He is anxious to do.

Truth Number One: The Impartiality of God

"Let him ask of God, that giveth to *all* men" (James 1:5). Thanks, I needed that! I sometimes wonder if God is aware of *my* situation. I see him dealing with everyone else's situation but somehow my problems seem unique.

Not to have what I need is forgivable, but if I do not believe God's promise to give me what I need, and I refuse to ask, He can hardly forgive my stubborn unwillingness.

Truth Number Two: The Individuality of God

"Who giveth to all men *liberally.*" The word "liberal" in the text has two meanings associated with it. The first meaning teaches us the *manner* by which God gives us His wisdom. The word actually means, "to stretch out," and it pictures God stretching or spreading out His table of wisdom and loading it down lavishly with every morsel of wisdom you can possibly imagine. The way God dispenses His wisdom to those who ask is by lavishly pouring out to them the full supply of that which they need.

Years ago, I heard a sermon on the familiar New Testament parable of the Prodigal Son. Only this time the preacher who delivered the message changed the title of the message to "The Prodigal Father." According to his understanding, the father was the one who best illustrated prodigality. He was the one who spared nothing in pouring out blessing upon his wayward son who returned home.

James teaches that when God dispenses His wisdom to us, He is the Prodigal Father. God always gives to us in "good measure, pressed down, shaken together, and running over" (Luke 6:38).

When Solomon asked for wisdom, God gave him what he wanted and added to it riches and honor.

But I said there were two meanings to the word "liberal." The first teaches us the manner of God's giving, the second teaches the *method* of His giving. The word "liberal" also is translated by the word "singly." It means that God answers my request for wisdom *individually*. I am excited to be included in God's promise to "all men," but I am overwhelmed when I realize that my request is not dealt with on a human production line, but in a special, personal, individual encounter with the all-wise God.

Truth Number Three: The Indulgence of God

I'm discovering as my children grow up that it's quite an adventure to travel and vacation as a family. One of the lessons that has been reinforced since moving to California could be expressed in a maxim that looks something like this: "The package price that pays for everything when you enter an amusement park is in force until you pass the first chocolate-covered banana stand." As a maxim, it probably won't make the bumper sticker category, but if you're the breadwinner in your family, you can say "Amen" to the statement.

Every popcorn stand, every ice cream wagon, every trinket house offers Dad an opportunity to lavish his giving spirit upon his family.

"Daddy, do you have any money?"

"Now, son, you know I wouldn't bring six people to Disneyland without any money."

"Can I have some?"

After the third or fourth round of that conversation, if you're a normal parent, you respond with something like, "Goodnight, boy, do you think I'm made of money? I don't hold a partial deed to Fort Knox! Do you have any idea how much it cost to get into this place?"

I doubt if there's a father or mother who hasn't responded in a similar fashion at some time in their parental career.

But get this! Our Father in heaven never responds to His children like that! Our text says that when we come to God asking for wisdom, "He upbraids us not." Literally, that means that He never scolds us for coming. No matter how often we approach Him, He gives us gently what we need. He does not reproach us or make us feel guilty.

God never uses guilt as a weapon in dealing with His children

. . . never! Sometimes He is presented in that light, but that is a sad misrepresentation.

I said earlier that once we understand the nature of God, we are encouraged to ask Him for wisdom. His impartiality, individuality, and indulgence are simple invitations to approach Him with our needs. But there's one more principle that we need to implement when we come to God for wisdom. Admit our need, acknowledge God as our source, and,

ASK IN FAITH

"But let him ask in faith, nothing wavering . . ." (James 1:6). The principle of "asking in faith" is not isolated to this passage. It is consistently presented throughout the New Testament Scriptures:

> And all things, whatever ye shall ask in prayer, believing, ye shall receive. (Matthew 21:22)

> Therefore, I say unto you, whatsoever things ye desire, when ye pray, believe that ye receive them, and ye shall have them. (Mark 11:24)

Martin Luther had a terrible time with the Book of James because he felt that the emphasis on *works* in the epistle contradicted his understanding of justification by faith. He called James a "strawy epistle." But after Martin Luther died, John Wesley came along and pointed out that though James emphasizes works, it also emphasizes faith. He noted that six verses into the epistle we are told to "ask in *faith*" (James 1:6), and that six verses from the end of the epistle we are told that "the prayer of *faith* shall save the sick" (James 5:15).

The prayer of faith is the prayer God answers. When we ask in faith, we believe God, we believe that His will is absolute, and we believe that what we have asked, He is ready and able to do. We pray and we expect the answer.

We become like the little boy who went to church one night and asked his pastor if he would have the congregation pray for his sick sister. The pastor said he would gladly do it. He announced the request to the congregation, and as they went to prayer, he saw the little boy run out of the back door of the church.

The congregation felt the young lad to be quite rude, leaving the service as soon as he had made his petition. But the next day as the preacher was chiding the youth, he got this explanation, "Oh, Pastor,

I wasn't rude. I ran home because I wanted to be the first one to see my sister well."

We are further instructed to pray in faith "nothing wavering." We are not to go to God with a battle raging within our souls between what our logic tells us and what our faith tells us. The word "wavering" is a word which is literally translated by the phrase "to separate out." Relating it to prayer, it actually means to separate out our requests. It describes a man who comes to God with two mental lists. The one list is made up of those things for which we are able to believe God. The other list catalogs the impossibilities of our life and for those things we don't pray. The word "waver" is written in such a way that in the language of the Bible, it actually communicates intensive action within itself . . . inner agitation.

Two illustrations are presented to describe such a worshipper. He is "like a wave driven by the sea" and he is "a double-minded man."

When doubt inhabits our prayers, we are like a wave of the sea. Paul uses the same illustration to describe immature believers in his letter to the Ephesians. He exhorted the Ephesian church to "Be no more children, tossed to and fro and carried about with every wind of doctrine" (Ephesians 4:14). That's the picture! It's a scene of instability . . . moving back and forth from faith to doubt.

It is possible in our praying to become spiritual paranoids. We become double-minded and unstable in all our ways. Literally, the text describes such a person as "double-souled." Such a person never settles down to one position.

I heard about a woman who was describing her husband to some friends: "At a theologically liberal meeting, he's a liberal; at a theologically conservative meeting, he's a conservative." "And what is he like at home?" they asked her. "He's a perfect demon!" she answered. It's not difficult to understand why. For, "No man can serve two masters, for either he will hate the one and love the other; or else he will hold to the one, and despise the other" (Matthew 6:24).

If you are caught up in this exercise in futility, you need to heed James' instruction:

> Draw near to God, and He will draw near to you. Cleanse your
> hands, ye sinners, and purify your hearts.   (James 4:8)

When we admit our need, acknowledge God as our source, and ask in faith believing, God promises that He will give us the wisdom we desire. He is not a "give-me" machine, or a heavenly bellhop, but when we follow His instructions He has promised to respond.

He is no less explicit in His promise to the doubter who prays. "For let not that man think that he shall receive anything of the Lord" (James 1:7). That is a very straight-forward reminder from the Word of God that some of our prayers are a waste of time.

Two Bible personalities illustrate the two approaches to God. Matthew 14 records the story of Peter's brief walk on the water. When he saw the Lord coming toward them on the water, he said, "Lord, bid me come unto thee." The Lord said, "Come." (Matthew 14:28-29)

Peter jumped out of the boat and confidently started toward the Savior. He was doing wonderfully well as long as he single-mindedly focused on the Lord. But when he saw the boisterous wind, he was afraid and he began to sink. A double-minded man is unstable in all his ways and shall *not receive* what he asks of God.

The second personality is Old Testament Job. Tried by the white-hot furnace of God's testing, Job was counseled by everyone to give up on God. Even his wife told him to "curse God and die."

Job's response was the response of faith. "Though He slay me, yet will I trust Him" (Job 13:15). "He knoweth the way that I take and when He has tried me, I shall come forth as gold" (Job 23:10).

We approach the Father as Peter or as Job. The choice is ours. We may come in doubt and be disappointed, or we may come in faith and receive. Before you read any further, stop for just a moment and ask God for the wisdom that you need from Him!

10

The Result of Wisdom In The Christian Life

One Saturday a football enthusiast was frantically repairing his television antenna on the sloped roof of his second-story home. As the four o'clock game time approached, he began to hurry his efforts to complete the chore so that he would not miss anything.

All of a sudden, he lost his footing and began to slide down the slippery tile toward the edge of the roof. As he was falling over the edge, he managed to grab the eaves trough in desperation. There, he hung by his fingers two stories above ground.

His first impulse was to seek help from ground level. "Can anybody down there help me?" he shouted, but everybody was inside, beyond reach of his cry.

Instinctively and as a last resort, he looked up toward heaven and called out, "Can anybody up there help me?" Out of the stillness of the afternoon, he heard a deep resonant voice respond with these instructions, "Believe and let go!"

After a reflective pause, he answered back, "Can anybody *else* up there help me?"

We chuckle at this obviously apocryphal story, but while we are laughing, we know that God is often our last resort, and when we do finally turn to Him for help, we hope that He does not ask us to do something which demands too much.

Our current investigation into God's working wisdom demands that we change that pattern of thinking. God cannot be last. He must be first. In fact, He must be first and last . . . and He must be everything in between.

In Paul's prayer for the Colossian believers, he put it this way,

"That you might be *filled* with the knowledge of His will in all wisdom and spiritual understanding" (Col. 1:9).

God's wisdom cannot be something we turn to only when we need help. God's wisdom is to be the motivating factor of our lives. It is to control our minds and our activities. It is to be the central focus of our lives.

The importance of wisdom in the Christian life is underscored by the fact that Paul saw godly wisdom as the greatest need of the Colossian church. The prayer which Paul prayed for the Colossians is especially significant because Paul prayed this prayer for a church he had never visited . . . for people he did not personally know.

Through a letter from his friend, Epaphras, he had learned of their needs . . . their problems and the challenges that they faced daily. With their particular situation in mind, he prayed, and these are the words of his prayer:

> For this cause we also, since the day we heard of it, do not cease to pray for you, and to desire that ye might be filled with the knowledge of His will in all wisdom and spiritual understanding; That ye might walk worthy of the Lord unto all pleasing, being fruitful in every good work, and increasing in the knowledge of God; Strengthened with all might, according to His glorious power, unto all patience and longsuffering with joyfulness; giving thanks unto the Father, which hath made us meet to be partakers of the inheritance of the saints in light; Who hath delivered us from the power of darkness, and hath translated us into the kingdom of His dear Son; in whom we have redemption through His blood, even the forgiveness of sins."
>
> (Colossians 1:9-14)

Though the prayer continues beyond this point, we will examine only this portion. In its entirety, this is one of the longest prayers in the New Testament. Except for the disciples' prayer in Matthew 6, and our Lord's high priestly prayer in John 17, I think this is the most important prayer recorded in the Bible.

The prayer is long, but the request is simple. In actuality, the prayer itself is contained in but one phrase, "That ye might be filled with the knowledge of His will in all wisdom and spiritual understanding." This phrase is the *request* . . . the rest of the passage describes the *result* of the request being fulfilled in the believers' lives.

Later on in Colossians, Paul's friend, Epaphras, rephrased Paul's request like this, "That ye may stand perfect and complete in all the will of God" (Colossians 4:12).

THE REQUEST

Although Paul did not know the Colossians, he was confident that their need would be met in God's wisdom alone. He prayed that they would be filled or controlled by that wisdom. He specifically terms this spiritual commodity, "the knowledge of His will in all wisdom and spiritual understanding" (Colossians 1:9).

It does not take much study to discover that the *will* of God and the *wisdom* of God are inseparably linked to the *Word* of God. In essence, Paul prays that the Colossian believers will be saturated and controlled by God's Word.

Writing to these same Colossians later in this letter, he instructed them, "To let the Word of God dwell in them richly" (Colossians 3:17). To the Ephesians, he wrote, "Be ye not unwise but understanding what the will of the Lord is . . ." (Ephesians 5:17).

What Paul recognized from this New Testament vantage point, the Psalmist saw from his perspective. David wrote:

> Blessed is the man . . . whose delight is in the law of the Lord.
> (Psalm 1:1-2)

The input of God's Word into the life of the believer is the irreducible minimum in the acquisition of wisdom. When Paul uses the term "wisdom" as a synonym for the "will of God," he means basically the *content* of God's Word. He uses a term which requires mental excellence at its highest level. He is talking about *learning* the concepts of God's Word.

But notice how Paul further qualifies his request by the use of the phrase, "spiritual understanding." If "wisdom" is the *acquisition* of knowledge from God's Word, then "*spiritual understanding*" is the *application* of knowledge from God's Word.

Actually the term, "spiritual understanding," refers to the process of *applying* God's truth to the situations of life. It is the very necessary, practical aspect of wisdom. Paul knew that the acquisition of knowledge would not be enough. If biblical knowledge is not useful to us in living our lives each day, then it is really of no value at all! Some of the definitions of wisdom I have uncovered have captured this thought. For instance, Cooleridge defined wisdom as, "Common sense in an uncommon degree." Spurgeon said that wisdom was "the right *use* of knowledge." A. T. Robertson explained it as, "The right *use* of one's opportunities in holy living." Ropes said that wisdom was, "The supreme and divine quality of the soul whereby man knows and *practices* righteousness." The apostle, James, taught that we show what kind of wisdom we have by the way we live. He wrote, "Who is a wise man and endued with knowledge among you? Let him show out of a good conversation his works with meekness of wisdom" (James 3:13). J. I. Packer agrees that wisdom "is the power to see, and the inclination to choose the best and highest goal, together with the surest means of attaining it."[1]

The New English Bible's translation of the familiar Romans 12:1, 2 makes this truth come alive:

> Let your minds be remade and your whole nature thus transformed. Then you will be able to discern the will of God, and to know what is good, acceptable and perfect.
>
> (Romans 12:2 NEB)

When I was a young boy growing up in the Baptist parsonage, I remember a situation that dramatically illustrates this aspect of wisdom. Our home, at this particular time, was located on the second floor of a huge garage that once belonged to a large estate. In order to get to the apartment, it was necessary to ring the doorbell at the ground level and be received by answering a buzzer which unlatched the door leading to the stairway.

During a particular time in our family's ministry at that church, I heard the doorbell ring in our apartment late almost every Saturday night. I learned from my father that our visitor was at one time a very successful pastor who had become an alcoholic.

On Saturday night after a full day of drinking, George would be overcome with guilt and seek help from my father. Dad told me that often when he would read the Scriptures to comfort and encourage this troubled man, that the man himself would begin to quote Scriptures in his drunken stupor. He actually knew vast portions of God's Word by memory, but obviously, he had not been able to make application to his own life. He knew the will of God in *"all wisdom"* but certainly not in all *"spiritual understanding."*

As we look about us in the church today, it is quite apparent that the *application* of God's truth is our greatest need. The difference between what we know and what we do is the reason for our powerless posture before the watching world. We resist the trite excuse of the "hypocrite within the church," but after we have done our best to defend ourselves against that accusation, we bow our heads in humble admission.

THE RESULT

In the last half of Paul's prayer for the Colossians, he documents the result of applied wisdom in the life of the believer. The result clauses provide five motivating reasons for giving one's life to the *acquisition* and *application* of God's truth.

If, as a Christian, you live out Paul's request, you will discover five dynamic dimensions in your life.

1. You Will Be Pleasing The Lord Constantly.

"That ye might walk worthy of the Lord unto all pleasing; (Colossians 1:10).

The Christian experience is likened, in the New Testament, to a step by step walk. Often we are encouraged to live or "walk" in light of our high calling as Christians:

> Walk worthy of the vocation where with ye are called.
> (Ephesians 4:1)

> Walk worthy of God, who hath called you into His kingdom
> and glory. 1 Thess. 2:12)

> We beseech you brethren and exhort you by the Lord Jesus that
> as ye have received of us how ye ought *to walk and to please
> God*, so you would abound more and more. (1 Thess. 4:1)

Paul's pertinent instruction to the Thessalonians summarizes the highest goal of the Christian experience, *"Walk and please God."* It is the will of the Father in heaven that every believer be able to say what His Son Jesus Christ said, "I do always those things that please Him . . ." (John 8:29).

But is that possible in this life on earth? The answer is a resounding, "Yes." The secret is locked up in this prayer.

> Be filled with the knowledge of his will of God in all wisdom
> and spiritual understanding *that* ye might walk worthy of the
> Lord unto *all* pleasing. (Colossians 1:10)

DYNAMIC DIMENSIONS OF CHRISTIAN LIFE	
WALK	**"Pleasing The Lord Constantly"**
WORK	**"Producing Fruit Consistently"**
WISDOM	**"Progressing In Knowledge Continually"**
WELFARE	**"Persevering In Stress Cheerfully"**
WORSHIP	**"Praising God Correctly"**

Paul said that it is possible for a Christian to so fill his life with God's Word that he can actually be constantly pleasing his Father in heaven.

Here's how it works. As you study God's Word you come to know God as a person in an intimate, wonderful way. As you know God personally, knowing what pleases Him becomes second nature. An intuitive, conscious awareness of His will takes over in your life.

I fear that we struggle far too much with "the will of God." If we knew Him better, we would not be so much in doubt about that which pleases Him. Our "will of God" crises gives us away. How can we be expected to anticipate the will of a stranger? We need to cultivate our knowledge of God so that we can comprehend the slightest nuance of God's perfect will.

For most of the years of my ministry, I have lived life in the fast lane. Many times, I have eaten meals on my way to an important appointment or speaking engagement. Often when my wife was planning to accompany me, I would pick her up at home on my way out of town. After we had been married for a number of years, I called Donna one day from the office and told her I would be home in a few minutes to pick her up for a trip to a neighboring city. As I pulled into the driveway, I honked the horn to encourage her to hurry. After waiting for a few minutes, I went inside to find Donna dressed and waiting for me, but rather displeased at my method of announcing my arrival. I have a feeling that had I not gone in to get her, I might still be waiting in the car. I learned something new about Donna that day. I have never repeated that mistake. The better you know someone, the better you know what pleases them!

Over the past few years, I have come to the firm conclusion that the toy manufacturers of America are out to drive parents insane. Their latest attempt to accomplish that goal has been the invention of electronic computer games. The hand-held ones, if you please! Last year as we started on our vacation, that "drive-you-crazy" noise of two computer games being played in the backseat began to get on my nerves. I can tell you honestly that my two boys are not at all in doubt about the use of computer games in the car on long trips. They have come to know their Dad so well that they know what pleases him.

I think you get my point. We must get to know God thoroughly through His Word, to please Him constantly.

2. You Will Be Producing Fruit Consistently.

"*Being fruitful in every good work . . .*" Colossians 1:10).

There is a direct relationship between the Word of God and fruitfulness. Paul has established this relationship already in this very chapter. He speaks in verses 5 and 6 of the "Word of the truth of the gospel, which is come unto you, as it is in all the world, *and bringeth forth fruit*" (Colossians 1:5-6).

Paul views the Word and wisdom of God as the key to a fruitful Christian life. There is much tunnel vision when it comes to bearing fruit. In actuality, fruit bearing touches on three basic areas of the Christian walk.

The Christian's Conduct

> What fruit had ye then in those things of which ye are now ashamed? For the end of those things is death. But now being made free from sin, and become servants of God, ye have your fruit unto holiness, and the end everlasting life.
>
> (Romans 6:21-22)

The fruit unto holiness speaks of the conduct and activity of the Christian's life.

The Christian's Converts

> Now I would not have you to be ignorant, brethren, that often-times, I purposed to come unto you (but was prevented thus far), *that I might have some fruit among* other Gentiles.
>
> (Romans 1:13)

Paul here speaks of his desire to win some of the Romans to Christ. This is the aspect of fruit bearing that is understood by the majority of Christians when the term "fruit bearing" is used. Though very important, it is only part of the whole.

The Christian's Character

> *But the fruit of the Spirit is love, joy, peace, longsuffering, gentleness, goodness, faith, meekness, self-control; against such there is no law.* (Gal. 5:22-23)

These qualities are character traits that are developed within the Christian by the filling of the Spirit and the filling of the Word of God.

The important concept here, however, is this. *All fruit is the direct: result of being filled with the will of God in all wisdom and spiritual understanding.* The promise of God's Word is clear. Let God's Word dominate your life and you will be a consistent, day-by-day, regular fruit-bearing believer. No more stops and starts, no more fits and jumps, no more ups and downs. It *is* possible to live beyond the uncertainties of life at a level of spiritual stability.

3. You Will Be Progressing In Knowledge Continually.

"Increasing in the knowledge of God" (Colossians 1:10).

The third result of being filled with God's Word and His wisdom is a gradual developing knowledge of God. An increase in the knowledge of God should be a high priority with every believer. The input of God's Word is the only avenue to that goal.

Peter championed this imperative as he wrote his second epistle. His last recorded words challenge us all:

> But grow in grace and in the knowledge of our Lord and Savior Jesus Christ. (2 Peter 3:18)

He said the same thing in his first epistle.

Add to your faith virtue and to your virtue, knowledge.

(1 Peter 1:5)

God places no premium on ignorance. While it is true that knowledge is never enough, it is also true that without knowledge there can be no growth in the believer's life. The current emphasis on experience as opposed to knowledge can never produce mature believers.

It is alarming, to say the least, to observe the biblical ignorance among Christians of our day. Not long ago, a Bible knowledge test was given to a major fundamental denomination. The test was administered to the graduating seniors of the high school department. The results of that test were so discouraging that the entire Bible curriculum came up for review.

One student said that the four leading disciples were Matthew, Mark, Luther and John. Another paper contained the news that Sodom and Gomorrah were lovers, and still a third graduate announced that the epistles were the wives of the apostles. As a pastor and a teacher I want to cry, but I am not yet ready to give that test to my congregation.

Our problem is like the problem of a man who deposits $100.00 in the bank with the idea that he can draw out $25.00 a week for the rest of his life. That's ridiculous, you say! And you are absolutely right. But it is no more ridiculous than the Christian who tries to live his whole adult life off the information he gained from his childhood Sunday school experience. In order for there to be progress in our understanding of God, there must be progress in our understanding of His Word.

When we make a commitment to be filled with God's Word, our growth in the knowledge of God is an automatic by-product.

4. You Will Be Persevering In Stress Cheerfully.

"Strengthened with all might according to his glorious power, unto all patience and longsuffering with joyfulness" (Colossians 1:11).

Here's where the rubber meets the road. Living joyfully in the midst of difficulty is the supreme reality test for Christians. Not long ago, I heard a radio announcer say something like this, "If you see someone who has a lot of problems and he still has a smile on his face . . . you can be sure he has found someone to blame it on."

But there just might be another explanation. He might be a

Spirit-filled, Word-controlled Christian. Paul says that when the Word of God controls our life, we are strengthened with all might according to God's glorious power with the result that we have patience and longsuffering *with* joy."

I have been observing as I read the New Testament that God views our need for power and might and strength in a much different manner than we do. We think we need God's power for the big things in life—the *big* projects, the *big* financial needs, etc! But God sees us as we are! He knows that we need the greatest input of His power for the daily grind and for the "patience and longsuffering" kinds of challenges. It's the *inner man*, not the *outer man* that fights the greatest battle. Listen to the great apostle as he prays for the inner needs of the Ephesian saints:

> That He (God) would grant you according to the riches of His glory to be strengthened with might by His Spirit in the inner man. (Ephesians 3:16)

The outward man is perishing, *but* the inner man can be renewed day-by-day through God's wonderful Word (2 Cor. 4:16).

Please note that the goal is not just enduring our difficulties. We are to triumph in them with all joyfulness. God is not interested in our making it through somehow. He has provided the means whereby we may experience what life throws at us with great victory and joy. Once again, that dynamic lifestyle is the direct result of God's wisdom controlling your life. An old adage puts it this way: "If you let the Word of God control your life you can become like the tea kettle, up to your neck in hot water, but still singing." Or, to put it another way, the Christian who is so controlled has learned how to enjoy the scenery along a detour.

5. You Will Be Praising God Correctly.

"*Giving thanks unto the Father*" (Colossians 1:12).

The last result of being filled with God's wisdom is a proper and scriptural prayer life. Paul says that a Word-filled believer will be naturally filled with praise and thanksgiving to God. His thanksgiving, however, will be along highly spiritual lines.

He is not seen here as being thankful for health or wealth or other physical blessings. He is viewed as being thankful for his spiritual heritage. The prayers of the New Testament consistently follow the same pattern. There is a glaring absence of the physical requests that dominate so much of our praying today.

The first item on Paul's suggested thanksgiving list is the *light* God has provided for all who believe. He says it this way in verses 12 and 13, "He (God) made us fit to be partakers of the inheritance of the saints in *light* . . . who hath delivered us from the power of *darkness.*"

Paul never forgot the transformation that took place in his own life. As a religious zealot, he groped in the darkness after God. One day God flooded his whole being with light. The light temporarily blinded him but permanently enlightened him. Whenever he prayed, he thanked God for the blessing of spiritual light.

Secondly, Paul gave thanks and encouraged the Colossians to give thanks for *love.* He said that God "translated us into the kingdom of his dear son" (v. 13). Paul's life, before he met the Lord, was characterized by hatred. He lived in the kingdom of hostility. He "breathed out threatenings and slaughter" (Acts 9:1). But when he met the Lord, he was translated out of the kingdom of hatred and into the kingdom of *love.*

A conquered people in Paul's day were often picked up in mass and removed to a totally different location and culture so as to prevent further uprisings and rebellion. In just the same way, Paul pictures the Christian as having been plucked out of the kingdom of hatred and set down in the new kingdom of *love* presided over by God's dear Son.

Paul concluded his praise list with a third blessing. He thanked God and urged the Colossians to thank God for *liberty* "*in* whom we have redemption through His blood" (Colossians 1:14).

Our redemption by the blood of Christ has set us free from the slavery of sin.

> But God be thanked, that whereas ye were the *servants of sin,* ye have obeyed from the heart that form of doctrine which was delivered you. Being, then, made free from sin, ye became the *servants of righteousness.* (Romans 6:17-18)

> Forasmuch as ye know that ye were not redeemed with corruptible things, like silver and gold, *from your vain manner of life* received by traditions from your fathers, but with the precious blood of Christ, as of a lamb without blemish and without spot. (I Peter 3:18-19)

We have been released from mandatory service to sin and the empty life that accompanied that service.

Finally, then, Paul inspires us to a wisdom-controlled life by reminding us that it will change our prayer life. We will know the joy of focusing our attention on the lasting realities of the spiritual realm.

These five dynamic results of God's wisdom in the believer's life are all encompassing. They touch every area of our relationship with God and with each other.

When we are pleasing the Lord constantly . . . that's our Christian walk.

When we are producing fruit consistently . . . that's our Christian work.

When we are progressing in knowledge continually . . . that's our Christian wisdom.

When we are persevering in stress cheerfully . . . that's our Christian welfare.

When we are praising God correctly . . . that's our Christian worship.

And what else can there be? God's wisdom literally *fills* our lives and controls every area of our whole being.

Several years ago, I had the opportunity to perform the wedding ceremony for two of the neatest young people I had ever met. They were on the Navigator's staff at Indiana University in Bloomington, Indiana. Their wedding turned out to be a church service. They both gave dynamic testimonies of their relationship with the Lord and of His leading in their lives. To this day, when I officiate at a wedding, I remember Bill and Rhonda's wedding.

About two years after their wedding, I received a call from Bill telling me that he and Rhonda had just returned from the doctor's office where they had learned that Rhonda had an advanced case of leukemia. What a shock! We prayed together over the phone, and a few days later we got together to discuss the ominous prognosis the doctor had given.

Rhonda went into remission briefly, but within a few months her condition began to deteriorate rapidly. She was finally admitted to the Indiana University Medical Center in Indianapolis, Indiana.

I will never forget the afternoon I flew to Indianapolis to visit her. My heart was heavy as I walked into her room. I wondered what

I would say to her. When I left the hospital, I had the distinct impression that I had been ministered to that day. Rhonda spent most of our visit sharing with me the things God had been teaching her through His word. She repeated some of the verses she and Bill had been memorizing together.

Just a few days after my visit, Rhonda went home to be with the Lord. In the hour before she died, she recited many of the passages of God's Word with which she had filled her life. According to the nurse who was with her when she died, "She went home to God in the middle of a verse."

What a way to die . . . but better yet, what a way to live! "Being filled with the wisdom of God in all wisdom and spiritual understanding" (Colossians 1:9).

NOTE

1. J. I. Packer, *Knowing God* (Downers Grove: InterVarsity Press, 1973), p. 93.